brilliant

essay

brilliant

essay

What you need to know and how to do it

Bill Kirton

Prentice Hall
is an imprint of

Harlow, England • London • New York • Boston • San Francisco • Toronto • Sydney • Singapore • Hong Kong
Tokyo • Seoul • Taipei • New Delhi • Cape Town • Madrid • Mexico City • Amsterdam • Munich • Paris • Milan

PEARSON EDUCATION LIMITED

Edinburgh Gate
Harlow CM20 2JE
Tel: +44 (0)1279 623623
Fax: +44 (0)1279 431059
Website: www.pearsoned.co.uk

First published in Great Britain in 2011

© Pearson Education 2011

The right of Bill Kirton to be identified as author of this work has been asserted
by him in accordance with the Copyright, Designs and Patents Act 1988.

Pearson Education is not responsible for the content of third party internet sites.

ISBN: 978-0-273-74375-0

British Library Cataloguing-in-Publication Data
A catalogue record for this book is available from the British Library

Library of Congress Cataloging-in-Publication Data
Kirton, Bill.
 Brilliant essay : what you need to know and how to do it / Bill Kirton.
   p. cm.
 Includes bibliographical references.
 ISBN 978-0-273-74375-0 (pbk.)
 1. English language--Rhetoric--Problems, exercises, etc. 2. Essays--
Authorship--Problems, exercises, etc. 3. Report writing--Problems, exercises,
etc. I. Title.
 PE1471.K57 2011
 808'.042--dc22
                                    2010044454

10 9 8 7 6 5 4 3 2 1
15 14 13 12 11

Typeset in 10/14pt Plantin by 30
Printed and bound in Great Britain by Henry Ling Ltd., at the Dorset Press,
Dorchester, Dorset

Contents

About the author

Before taking early retirement to become a full-time writer, **Bill Kirton** was a lecturer in French at the University of Aberdeen. He has also been a Royal Literary Fund Writing Fellow at the RGU in Aberdeen, and the universities of Dundee and St Andrews. His radio plays have been broadcast by the BBC and on the Australian BC. His crime novels and a historical novel have been published in the UK and USA and his short stories have appeared in several anthologies. He lives in Aberdeen with his wife, Carolyn.

His website is www.bill-kirton.co.uk and his blog can be found at http://livingwritingandotherstuff.blogspot.com/

Author's acknowledgements

I owe a lot to the students I've worked with over the years. I hope I taught them some things; I know they taught me many. So let me acknowledge at the start my appreciation of the interesting and stimulating discussions I shared with them. More specifically in the context of this volume, I'd like to thank Steve Cook and others at the Royal Literary Fund who initiated and ran the imaginative scheme which funded Writing Fellowships in universities throughout the UK. It was through that scheme that I met Kathleen McMillan and Jonathan Weyers, who became friends as well as colleagues. My thanks to them for their expertise, knowledge, experience and friendship.

Finally, Steve Temblett, Katy Robinson, Emma Devlin and Rhian McKay at Pearson Education have been unfailingly kind and cooperative and I'm truly grateful to them for all their help.

Publisher's acknowledgements

Brilliant Essay draws on the research and writings of Kathleen McMillan and Jonathan Weyers as published in *How to Write Essays and Assignments*.

The dictionary entry on page 202 is reproduced from *The Penguin A–Z Thesaurus* (Penguin Books 2000, 2001, 2007). Copyright © Penguin Books, 2000. Reproduced by permission of Penguin Books Ltd.

The publisher is grateful to the British Standards Institution for permission to reproduce the proofreading symbols shown in Figure 16.1.

In some instances we have been unable to trace the owners of copyright material, and we would appreciate any information that would enable us to do so.

Introduction: do as we say, not as we do

To explain why we chose that heading for the introduction, let's start with a question. What's wrong with these sentences (all of which you'll find in this book)?

1 Finally, two examples illustrating a common error.

2 But the more familiar you become with your subjects and the issues being covered in your course, the faster you'll be able to read.

3 It'll help you to understand what's being conveyed.

4 ... a word that links adjective clauses to the noun they're referring to.

5 ... something to base your thinking and writing on.

The main answer is that they all break rules (of grammar, punctuation and style) which we'll be saying must *never* be broken. (As does that sentence, too, because we're not 'saying' anything, we're 'writing' it.) More specifically: 1 isn't a sentence because there's no verb in it; 2 begins with a conjunction, i.e. a word which should join two parts of a sentence, not start it; 3 uses contractions ('It'll' and 'what's'); and 4 and 5 both end with a preposition.

Another question – this time about the whole problem of political correctness and gender-specific language. When we give examples involving a student or lecturer, do we say he or she? Or do we stay correct and use the either/or form, writing sentences such as 'The student must ensure that he or she conducts his or her research in a style that suits himself or herself'? We hope the answer to that one is self-evident.

We're starting with these questions to warn you against copying the style of this book in your academic writing; it breaks many of the rules which you'll need to respect. The reason for that is that our aim here isn't to be academic or formal; we want our style to be personal, conversational, direct and easy to read. So we don't mind starting paragraphs with 'OK', or sentences with 'And' or 'But'. We'll be using the sort of contractions familiar in everyday speech, such as 'you'll', 'we've' and 'don't'. We don't want the writing to be sloppy or to give you examples of 'bad' English but nor do we want to be constrained by the formality of conventional academic style.

So that's why we've used the 'incorrect' formulae in the sentences we quoted. And the way we'll overcome the gender-specific issue is by using 'he' or 'she' at random. Students and lecturers alike will sometimes be male, sometimes female. There'll be no attempt to make sure there's a 50-50 split to guarantee political correctness either. Our intention throughout isn't to be 'correct' but to communicate.

The book is organised into six parts. The first part focuses on the importance of writing, the things markers are looking for and how to get started. Part 2 is about planning your research and the importance of critical thinking, while Part 3 deals with writing your first draft. In Part 4 we look at the various aspects of writing techniques, including grammar, punctuation, vocabulary and structure. Part 5 moves on to editing, revision, plagiarism and referencing; and the final part stresses the importance of presentation, suggests ways to improve your marks and considers the special challenges of exam essays.

You'll find that some points, such as those concerning referencing and plagiarism, the need to stay objective, and the importance of using evidence to support your arguments, are repeated quite frequently. We've done this deliberately whenever we feel something needs to be stressed or re-stressed.

If, when you've read the book, it's helped you to feel more confident about things, we've achieved our goal. University is a great foundation for your future and the various aspects of it, including the writing you do there, will help you to develop and demonstrate your abilities as well as find out more about yourself in the process.

PART 1

Establishing
the basics

Developing good writing skills

Some students experience a sinking feeling at the prospect of having to write an essay or assignment. Others see it as a challenge. Our intention in this book is to eliminate the first response and highlight the second to help you approach such tasks with more confidence and a better understanding of the purpose they serve. On the surface, that purpose seems simple – you're being asked to organise and communicate your knowledge and understanding of a particular topic. But the process of gathering material, then shaping it into an argument will help to improve your language and communication skills and develop critical thinking techniques that you'll keep on using long after you've graduated.

The importance of writing effectively

It must be obvious that, if you can generate ideas and communicate them well on paper, you have a talent that you'll be able to apply in all sorts of contexts, well beyond your student days. So, while writing may seem to be just a regular university chore, in fact it's one of the most important skills you'll take away with you when you leave. Attitudes to it vary but, whether you consider yourself competent or have doubts about your abilities, the need to produce assignments will help you to learn and refine your own writing into an effective communication tool.

Identifying the basics

Let's start by spelling out the bare bones of the writing process.

First, you need something to write about. The essay question will indicate an area of interest and perhaps some specific aspects of it, so your job will be to look through information on that topic and choose relevant material.

Next, depending on what you've been asked to do, the material has to be sorted, organised and structured into an outline of your argument.

Once you've done that, you have to expand the outline into a flowing, coherent text. And to do so, you need to be able to 'play' with language. You obviously need to get your grammar, punctuation and spelling right, but you also need to choose and group your words into sentences and paragraphs that offer the best possible presentation of your material.

The final task is to read your essay carefully, correct any errors and improve it where it doesn't seem quite right.

The aim of all that is to group your ideas logically, show that you can use language flexibly to convey your thoughts clearly and, equally importantly, keep the reader's attention and interest.

brilliant tip

Sometimes, writing seems difficult because you're trying to write and work out the logic of an argument at the same time. It's much easier if you know where you're going. So, before you start, plan the structure of the whole text. That way, you'll always know where you are and you can focus on structuring individual sentences and paragraphs.

'Playing' with language

By 'playing' with language we mean being prepared to move things around and try out different word arrangements. People are often surprised at how writing can be changed and improved simply by rearranging the order of words or phrases.

Heads and tails

If you experiment by shifting elements around in a sentence, you can sometimes make it clearer and much more powerful. Moving a phrase or clause from the tail end to the beginning or vice versa often alters the emphasis and gives prominence to the aspect that needs to be stressed. Consider this statement:

The medical profession spent time and energy on activities in which they had little expertise because they were faced with the need to deliver a complete range of services with a greater attention to cost control as a result of the administration's directive.

It's too long, it just adds one bit of information after another and it leaves a muddled impression. The reader has little idea of which of the various elements is more important than the others. In the end, it all just tails weakly away. So let's move things about:

Faced with the need to deliver a complete range of services with a greater attention to cost control as a result of the directive, the medical profession spent time and energy on activities in which they had little expertise.

It's still too long but it's slightly better. At least now we've separated it into two distinct elements – the things that are causing the problems and the way the profession responds to them. But it's still unwieldy; the first half, for example, gives the reader no chance to pause and just keeps piling element upon element. Let's give it one more try:

The result of the directive was that the medical profession, faced with the need to deliver a complete range of services with a greater attention to cost control, spent time and energy on activities in which they had little expertise.

It's the best so far. The various elements have been brought into better relationships by starting with the directive, then wrapping its requirements inside the main point, which is the fact that the medics were doing things they knew little about. We could go on tweaking it, but we've done enough to make the point, which is to show how taking identical elements and rearranging them changes meaning and emphasis.

Long and short sentences

People often ask whether the length of sentences matters. The answer is 'that depends', but it's fairly obvious when sentences need changing because they just don't feel or sound right. Let's see how lengthening or shortening them affects their impact on the reader. We'll take what we called 'the best so far' from the examples above:

The result of the directive was that the medical profession, faced with the need to deliver a complete range of services with a greater attention to cost control, spent time and energy on activities in which they had little expertise.

It's still one long sentence. Let's split it:

The directive required a complete range of services to be delivered with a greater attention to cost control. The result was that the medical profession spent time and energy on activities in which they had little expertise.

Perhaps this does make it clearer by allowing the reader to pause between the two separate pieces of information and absorb them separately. On the other hand, the separation destroys the power of the link (and implied conflict) between the two.

And if you think a lot of shorter sentences would be easier to understand, try this:

The directive required a complete range of services to be delivered. It also insisted on greater attention being paid to cost control. The medical profession had little expertise in this. As a result, they wasted time and energy on it.

That staccato effect is as bad as, maybe even worse than the original long, rambling effort, so there's no obvious rule about long is bad, short is good. Again, though, the point is that when you've written something, come back to it later and see whether you can improve your message by moving its component parts around.

brilliant tip

There's great satisfaction in finding exactly the right combination of words to express what you want to say. That's fine when you have plenty of time to rework your draft text but it's not so easy in exams. You'll find, though, that taking that sort of care with your essays during your coursework will make sentence manipulation more instinctive and help you cope better with the pressure of time in the exam.

Writing and thinking

When you write, you're putting yourself on the page. Your manipulation of ideas, your choice of words, the fluidity of your text – all these things reflect your intellectual abilities. In other words, they demonstrate the quality of your thinking. They show that you can:

- solve problems and explain how you did so
- build and sustain arguments and counter-arguments

- understand the higher-order thinking of others, and apply it in your own work
- express opinions based on a sound analysis, synthesis and evaluation of many different sources.

Communicating

You should think of writing as performing two main functions: giving shape to your thoughts, and communicating those thoughts to others. With that in mind, it's obvious that you don't write an essay in the same way that you text a friend, nor do you write in the same way you speak. It's a question of what's called register.

Spoken language, texting, emails and messages to friends are all much more informal and relaxed than the register you need to use for academic writing. (So, incidentally, is the register we're using for this book, as we explained in the introduction.)

Using an informal register for your assignments will lose you marks for a variety of reasons.

- Informal language is limited, imprecise and often uses slang expressions which can quickly become dated and obsolete.
- It's more likely to be emotive and subjective.
- It may suggest that you're not taking the essay seriously. (On the other hand, writing convoluted sentences full of big 'impressive' words can be just as bad in terms of effective communication.)
- Thinking about your words and constructing your sentences and paragraphs to suit the understanding and ability of the person who'll be reading them is more likely to communicate ideas well. It'll probably get you better marks, too.

> ### brilliant tip
>
> Very few people can produce a fluent, error-free text at the first go. There's usually something that could be improved. Being self-critical is part of the writing process but you could also ask a 'study buddy', friend or member of your family to read your work critically and say whether it makes sense to them. They may pick out faulty logic, gaps, awkward passages or other things that don't seem right to them, even if they aren't exactly sure what the problem is.

Strategies for improving your writing

The obvious advice is practise, practise, practise, and the need to hand in regular pieces of work will make that easier. But writing calls for different skills – observation, listening, reading critically, and so on. Here are some tips to help you increase your awareness of what's needed.

Be sensitive to different registers

Essays and professional reports are formal documents. Have a careful, detailed look at your writing to make sure that your language and structures are well suited to the more formal style and vocabulary expected at university.

Learn to recognise the styles in your subject area

People often assume that different disciplines use different styles. Well, it's obviously true that the content of essays or articles will be different but there'll be few stylistic variations. Academic writing in all the disciplines uses good, clear, unambiguous standard English. Clear writing doesn't necessarily need long words, long sentences and long paragraphs. So look at how the experts in your field write and analyse their books and articles to see how they make their points and what makes their writing powerful and expressive.

Find out what register your target profession uses

Part of what you'll do at university will be preparation for writing in your professional life when you graduate. You'll find that different firms and organisations have their own 'house style' and, if you join them, you'll need to adapt to it. The same is true of the different professions. You can check this by looking at publications such as in-house journals, reports or printed publicity.

Try consciously to expand your vocabulary

You'll need to have a good command of the specialist terminology, or jargon, used in your specific field, but that's only part of what we mean. If you want to express ideas with clarity, force, subtlety and confidence, you'll need a wide vocabulary. If you have only a limited number of words at your disposal, your ability to express subtleties and nuances will be severely restricted. The more you read, the more words you'll acquire.

Find out what markers expect

As well as absorbing these apparently abstract comments about thinking, communicating, subtlety and so on, there are other, more fundamental things you can do. Markers expect clear thinking, good structure and the rest, but they also appreciate grammatically correct English, with words spelt properly and good punctuation. These are all aspects of good presentation so it's worth spending time learning about them and becoming more confident in how you use them. A little effort in these areas can have a noticeable effect on your grades.

What next?

Look at some of your recent work ...

... and compare it with exercises you wrote some time ago. Ask yourself if it's evolving as your studies progress, identify any changes and think about what you can do to make it more expressive and effective.

Learn more about language ...

... by writing for your university students' newspaper or joining a creative writing class. They'll both help you to see how flexible language can be and how it works in different genres. As well as helping you to develop as a writer, it'll give you constructive feedback from other more experienced writers.

Think about the type of writing ...

... you'll do in your chosen job. Look at job adverts in professional journals or national newspapers and notice how often they ask for 'good communication skills'. If you can confidently tell potential employers that you have the writing skills they need and show them evidence to prove it, you'll obviously improve your chances of an interview.

brilliant recap

- Good writing helps to generate and communicate ideas.
- Choose and structure your content to increase its impact and accessibility.
- Demonstrate the quality of your thinking in your writing.
- Choose your words and style to suit the audience.
- Writing calls for different skills: observation, listening, reading critically, and practice, practice, practice.

CHAPTER 2

Giving markers what they want

Your lecturers and tutors set tasks which spell out the aspects of a topic they want you to focus on and direct you to do it in a particular way (discuss, analyse, compare, etc.). The first and most obvious way of giving markers what they want is to do what the question asks. But there's more to it than that. They want to be sure that you understand the topic and are capable of analysing and presenting it in a coherent, persuasive way. In order to give you a better chance of satisfying their criteria, as we look at the specifics of what they want, we'll also identify what they don't want.

The three dimensions – presentation, structure, content

These are the three general areas that markers examine. They look for specific skills but they're also influenced by other factors which are less easy to define. Before we consider them, let's look at the broader criteria you'll be expected to meet. You'll find them in your course guide or handbook.

Course guides and handbooks

These may be issued as booklets or posted on your course module in your institution's virtual learning environment (VLE). In them you'll usually find general information, such as:

- Marking scales (often with details of the criteria you must meet to achieve the various levels).
- The citation and referencing formats you should use.
- Details of word limits (and whether appendices are included in the word count).
- Information about presentation and submission.
- Penalties for handing work in late.

Some also have basic advice on the writing style and conventions that may apply in your discipline.

Learning objectives

As well as noting those basics, you should look closely at your syllabus and what are known as learning objectives or outcomes – in other words, what a particular course is designed to teach you. Ideally, the way you're assessed should be connected with such outcomes. The learning objectives may be for the whole course, for specific themes within it, or both. Getting a clear idea of what your course is trying to teach you will help you to keep your assignments focused.

brilliant questions and answers

Q Who'll mark my work?

A Well, it's not always the person who gave the relevant lectures but it will be someone who's an expert in the field with a good knowledge of the subject. Papers may be 'double-marked' anonymously, which means they're marked by a second marker, usually from your department. If it's a degree exam mark or if the two markers give different grades, the paper may be sent to an external marker for a final decision.

Q **How do markers decide on what grade to give me?**

A This depends on several things, which may differ from subject to subject and assignment to assignment. Almost all markers have done lots of marking and they base their judgements on that and on their professional experience and expertise as academics. But to make sure that they remain objective and treat all students equally, they'll base their assessments on agreed (departmental) marking criteria. Sometimes, there'll be a marking scheme for a specific question, which will decide how many marks will be allocated to each part of your submission.

Marking criteria

Unfortunately, as with many other aspects of writing essays, there isn't a one-size-fits-all rule. Criteria differ from module to module, discipline to discipline and level to level. That's why it's important to identify those which are relevant for the piece of work you're doing and read them carefully to find out what's expected of you.

brilliant example

A typical top-band module assignment might outline what's needed by saying that the work should:

- Contain all the information required with no or very few errors or irrelevant material.
- Show evidence that you've read the relevant literature and used it effectively in your answer.
- Address the question correctly, understanding all its nuances.
- Demonstrate a full understanding of the topic within a wider context.
- Show good critical and analytical skills.
- Contain evidence of sound independent thinking.
- Express ideas clearly and concisely.
- Use an appropriate written structure and good English.
- Present diagrams, where required, that are detailed and relevant.

Degree classifications

Although there may be differences between institutions, there's a conscious effort to apply the same standards throughout higher education. As we've said, you'll find details in your course guide but honours degree grades will probably be awarded in line with the following general principles:

- **First (Grade A, numerically 70–100%)**
  - An outstanding command of the material, a high level of the awareness of issues, developments and critical dimensions of the subject material.
  - Original thinking and analysis, and evidence of clear relationships between the topic and the wider context of the discipline.
  - High standards in citations from the relevant literature.

- **Upper Second (B, 60–69%)**
  - A good level of knowledge and analysis with critical appraisal of important issues supported by appropriate reference to the literature.
  - Sophisticated argument and logical evaluation of the material.
  - A high standard of presentation.

- **Lower Second (C, 50–59%)**
  - Sound knowledge of subject material.
  - Too much description, not enough deeper critical thinking.
  - Evidence of some analysis but it lacks sophistication.

- **Third (D, 40–49%)**
  - Limited evidence of knowledge and understanding of the subject material.
  - Lack of analysis and evaluation of information and evidence.

  – Reliance on repeating factual material and descriptive or narrative presentation.

● **Fail (F, 35–39%)**

  – Inadequate understanding of the task.

  – No coherent argument.

  – No use of evidence from the relevant literature.

Anonymous marking

You'll normally see the marker's name on a feedback sheet or the notes on your essay so it's the student, not the marker, who's anonymous. The idea of this is to make sure that there's no bias in an assessment. Instead of your name, you put your Personal Identification or Matriculation number on your submission, so the marker knows nothing about your gender, ethnicity, age or academic record. That way, she has no preconceptions about the piece of work and it gets graded only on its merits.

brilliant tip

Although degrees have the classifications we've described, your coursework won't necessarily be graded in the same way. The tendency, though, is for students and staff still to think of work in terms of the degree categories. In broad terms, the different grades might be described as Excellent (First class), Very good (Upper Second), Good (Lower Second), Satisfactory (Third). Thereafter the descriptions may be Marginal fail, Clear fail and Bad fail.

Good presentation

Just think what it must be like to read and mark lots of responses to any set assignment and you'll get an idea of how grateful the marker will feel when he reads one in which the ideas are expressed clearly in good prose and which makes it easy to follow the writer's train of thought. Content and structure are important, but they won't have the desired impact unless they're properly presented. So be professional, make sure you check grammar, spelling, punctuation and style, and take time to edit and proofread your final draft carefully.

Things to avoid

Look out for features that can create a bad impression in the reader (marker). The main ones (with indications of which of our chapters deal with them in brackets) are:

- Clichés (Chapter 10).
- Colloquial language (Chapter 10).
- Subjectivity (Chapter 10).
- Poor sentence structure (Chapter 11).
- Lack of agreement (Chapters 10 and 12).
- Mixed-up tenses (Chapter 12).
- Weak punctuation (Chapter 13).
- Bad spelling (Chapter 14).

The final submission

Keep your writing objective, formal, and use clear, correct, standard English with no lapses into text-messaging speak or other inappropriate abbreviations. Make sure that, when you're printing it out, it follows standard typing conventions in terms of spacing, justification and punctuation. Not many institutions accept handwritten work now but, if yours does, make sure it's tidy. Never use capitals throughout.

Use grammar and spellcheckers with care. In spelling these can't distinguish between words that sound the same but have different spelling, or words that are specific to your subject and may have been misspelt in the text. There's no substitute for a close reading of your text.

Some of the grammatical 'errors' that are highlighted by checkers aren't errors at all. They're suggestions that you might want to try a different construction. This is especially true of the passive (see Chapter 10), which is commonly used in academic writing but which grammar checkers always seem to question.

Good structure

Structure is how you organise your ideas and arguments to present them as clearly and logically as possible in a sequence that makes sense. It's important at the level of sentences and paragraphs as well as at the overall level of the text itself. The sentences should be precise and well structured to emphasise the important points, the paragraphs should lead into and out of one another in an order that's easy to follow and be linked by sentences which keep the reader orientated.

The basics

If you make your introduction identifiable and coherent, it'll tell the reader what to expect in terms of the structure of the main body and he'll be grateful for the clarity. Then, if you continue to signpost your various points, guide him through the logic of how they link together, highlight your analysis of a particular problem, use comparisons and contrasts to convey your information, you'll keep his attention and make the read easier and more interesting. Finish it off with a tightly summarised analytical conclusion and you've given yourself a good chance of getting a positive response and the mark you deserve.

Initial planning is important to make sure your overall structure is logical. After that, construct your sentences and organise your paragraphs to support and convey that structure. If the reader comes across a poorly constructed sentence, he'll have to stop to work it out and he may lose the thread of your argument. And even though you may be expressing a personal viewpoint and using material to support it, be careful to keep it objective; don't make value judgements.

If you're expected to present any evidence in a visual format, make sure that all tables, diagrams, graphs or figures are properly labelled and appear in the text in a logical way and close to the point when you refer to them.

brilliant tip

In many disciplines, you'll need to refer to important works in the existing literature to support your argument. If you don't, or if you do but you fail to explain their significance, you'll weaken your case. You'll get credit for making such connections in your text, but don't plagiarise.

Good content

Markers want you to show knowledge but don't want to see just a list of facts. They want to see how you understand, use and arrange these facts to deal with the task you've been set. So an important part of your content must be an analysis of your supporting evidence. A description or narrative based on lecture notes or snippets you found on the internet won't do; you need to test knowledge, understand it and show how it relates to the question.

You also need to support your analysis with citations from a variety of primary and secondary sources, using a recognised citation and referencing system. But don't make the mistake of thinking that a string of direct quotations or quotations with a few of the original words changed will impress. It won't. The marker's looking to see how you use them to support your own ideas.

Make it relevant

Stick to the topic as it's set. Adding information just because you've read it or remembered it is pointless and counter-productive. It'll interrupt the flow of your argument and introduce ideas with no relevance to what you're doing. Equally, don't just use 'safe', general material – look at the deeper, more complex issues, and analyse and synthesise ideas to build an original argument.

Use feedback to help you to improve

You'll get feedback, written and oral, from your lecturers and you should use it to improve your written work. If the comments aren't clear, or you don't understand why you got the mark you did, ask the marker about it.

brilliant tip

Don't underestimate the importance of proofreading. You must learn to read your own written work critically. In coursework, set aside a decent period near the submission date for final editing, correcting and proofreading. In exams, time is short, but you should still make this an essential part of your strategy. It could make a big difference to your marks.

A checklist for your assignment

Presentation

- Find out whether you're allowed to use sub-headings. They'll help you to structure your content and organise your thoughts. If they're not allowed, use them for your first draft and delete them in the final one.

- Create a glossary of subject-specific terms that you'll probably need to use in your essay. You can refer to it as you write to make sure you spell terms correctly and you're not misusing them.

Structure

- Structure your essay. Don't just start writing and ramble on in a 'stream of consciousness' way.

- Make sure what you're writing is relevant to the task set.

- Don't describe, analyse.

- Use signpost words to help you and your reader to follow a logical path through your work.

Content

- Make sure you get your facts right.

- Interpret the subject for yourself. The marker wants to read your analysis, not notes you've taken in a lecture. Remember, in most subjects, there are no 'right' or 'wrong' answers, only good or bad ones.

What next?

Check out the marking scales …

… and criteria for your university or department/school and use that information to look at your recent grades and identify ways you could improve them.

Construct plans ...

... for your assignments. Make sure you break questions down into their various parts and interpret them carefully. By doing that you'll already be creating the elements of your plan and you'll just have to arrange and adapt them as you brainstorm fresh ideas on the topic.

Look over a piece of your writing ...

... that's already been marked by one of your lecturers. Read the feedback (on presentation, structure and content), note any points that might apply to future assignments, and use that knowledge when you begin working on them.

 brilliant recap

- Be sure of what markers expect of you in order to increase your chances of getting better grades.

- Check the criteria you're expected to meet in your course guide or handbook.

- Understand the importance of good presentation, structure and content.

- Use a checklist to identify the principal points in these three main areas and to check you've covered them effectively.

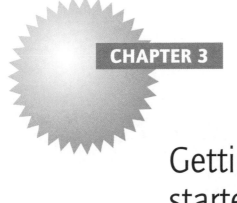

CHAPTER 3

Getting started with academic writing

I t may seem an obvious thing to say but writing and thinking are very closely allied. You'll find that assignments at university expect you to write in different forms, forms which are dictated by the type of thinking the question asks you to do. So here we'll look at the first stages of getting and organising material to plan the structure of your submission.

First steps

All writing exercises are designed to ask you three questions:

1 How well do you know and understand a topic?
2 How skilled are you at researching a specific aspect of it?
3 Can you organise information and evidence in a structured way to articulate and support your arguments?

Time management

If you're well organised you won't have experienced the feeling of panic that suddenly arises when you realise you have to hand in an essay by a particular day and time and you haven't even started thinking about it. On the other hand, if you're not, the feeling will be all too familiar. Let's face it, you're going to have to do the work and get it in on time, so it makes sense to organise your timetable to make sure that you can complete the task with as little stress as possible.

You'll find the submission date in the course handbook so it's easy to work out how long you've got before you have to hand in an assignment. Do that and then, according to the way you prefer to work, try to break that time down into segments, each of which you allocate to a particular activity. The sequence might be:

- working out what's being asked
- thinking about it and jotting down some ideas
- consulting lecture and tutorial notes or online resources
- doing some preliminary reading
- organising the material you've collected
- doing any additional reading that's necessary
- writing the first draft
- doing other things to get some distance between you and the work
- reviewing and rewriting
- editing, proofreading and printing out or writing the final copy.

Leave yourself extra time for the unexpected and don't forget that during the same period you'll be going to other lectures, doing more reading for different topics, relaxing and having to meet other commitments.

Breaking down the task

It's worth taking time to make sure you understand exactly what you're being asked to do. So, once again, ask yourself some questions.

What's the instruction?

We tend always to speak of 'essay questions' but many assignments are not questions but instructions. They're introduced by a word which is telling, not asking, you to do something – 'Describe', 'Analyse', 'Assess', 'Consider', etc. So the first thing to do is make sure you interpret the word properly.

What's the topic?

This may be obvious but it's worth making sure you identify exactly the specific topic and its context. It's all too easy to see a particular word or expression and jump to conclusions about what's being asked. Your job is to stick to the topic, not wander off on some personal interpretation of just one element of it.

What's the aspect of the topic?

Most topics have many facets and trigger lots of different opinions and responses. Make sure you understand and can define the specific focus that the person who set the assignment is asking you to apply.

What restriction is imposed on the topic?

Even though you've identified the precise aspect, there may be elements of the question that limit it or ask you to consider it in the light of other things. These things restrict the area in which you can operate.

As you do this preliminary breakdown of the task, it's worth jotting down your decisions. That'll help you identify the parameters within which you need to stay and it'll stop you wandering wherever your thinking takes you. You'll stick to the point. It's also the first step towards deciding how you'll approach structuring your response. All of which adds up to time well spent and, in the end, time saved.

brilliant example

The assignment is: 'Assess the importance of post-operative care in the rehabilitation of orthopaedic patients'.

The instruction tells you to 'assess' the topic, which is 'post-operative care'. The particular aspect of it is not its cost, effectiveness, desirability or anything else; it's its 'importance'. But that doesn't mean its overall importance in society or to every post-operative patient. In this case there are two restrictions which help to narrow the field of research: its value in the 'rehabilitation' of 'orthopaedic patients'.

Instruction words

Instruction words vary from subject to subject. As a general guide, we can suggest that they're asking you to do one (or more) of four things:

1 **Do**: create something, draw up a plan, calculate.
2 **Describe**: explain or show how something appears, happens or works.
3 **Analyse**: look at all sides of an issue.
4 **Argue**: look at all sides of an issue and provide supporting evidence for your position.

We obviously can't give an exhaustive list but some of the more common ones are as follows:

Account for	Give reasons for
Analyse	Give an organised answer looking at all aspects
Apply	Put a theory into operation
Assess	Decide on value/importance
Comment on	Give your opinion

Compare [with]	Discuss similarities and differences; draw conclusions on common areas
Compile	Make up (a list/plan/outline)
Consider	Describe/give your views on the subject
Contrast	Discuss differences/state your own view
Demonstrate	Show by example/evidence
Discuss	Give your own thoughts and support your opinion or conclusion
Evaluate	Decide on merit of situation/ argument
Exemplify	Show by giving examples
Explain	Give reason for – say why
Give an account of	Describe
Illustrate	Give examples
Outline	Describe basic factors
Review	Write a report/give facts and views on facts
Show	Demonstrate with supporting evidence
Specify	Give details of something
State	Give a clear account of ...

The topic

Once you're sure that you've pinpointed exactly what's being asked of you, it's time to start generating ideas about it. A good way to begin is by making a map of some brainstorming. Jot down thoughts as they occur, link them to other associated thoughts, try to think of points of view contrary to them. All you're doing is jotting down some headings which you can expand later through more thinking or extra reading. The headings may also be the beginnings of a structure but, at the moment, simply write whatever occurs to you. But be careful, don't be tempted to wander into areas which are outside the topic and the restrictions. The important thing about this is that what's on the page are your ideas and not those taken from books or lectures. Your reading may have influenced them, of course, but they're your own initial responses to the task. They arise from you doing some critical thinking.

Research

Now that you have some initial material on paper, it's time to start developing it further and adding more detail. You're ready to move to the research phase. Thanks to the initial brainstorming, you already have a few areas you need to investigate so you can narrow your focus to concentrate on them.

Reading lists

An obvious first source is your reading list. There you'll find both basic and more detailed texts. You don't really have to read all of them but they're valuable, targeted resources and you're bound to find material which is relevant to your topic there.

brilliant tip

If there's time, reading whole books will obviously be useful but in the case of reading for a particular assignment, it makes more sense to read selectively. Look at the contents page and the index to find the relevant sections.

Handouts/PowerPoint slides

Since the topic of your assignment is probably related to something that's been dealt with in lectures, it's likely that you'll find key issues and ideas, problems and solutions in the information provided by the lecturer.

Lecture notes

Get into the habit of writing the lecturer, topic and date on each of your lecture notes. It'll make it so much easier for you to find the relevant information later.

General or subject encyclopaedias

These can give you a quick insight into background information and also help to point you towards more detailed texts. Electronic versions may be available through your university library.

Library resources

You can use the electronic catalogue to find books and/or articles on your topic. It's also useful to look at the shelves devoted to the specific thing you're researching. You may come across titles which weren't suggested as fitting your search words but which may be relevant for you. The library's website will also help you to access electronic sources such as ebrary and e-journals.

Whichever of these resources you're using, it's another example of applying critical thinking. As you read and make your notes, you're making choices, deciding what's relevant and what's not, spotting arguments for and against a point of view. And the more you do that, the better you'll understand the topic and the clearer your ideas will become. You'll be looking for facts, examples, information to support a particular viewpoint, counter-arguments to balance your analysis, and your initial brainstorm will be growing accordingly, but always within the scope of the task which you identified at the start.

brilliant tip

If you're stuck, try asking the basic questions which trainee journalists are advised to use:

- Who's involved?
- What are the problems/issues?
- When, where, why and how did it all (or will it all) happen?

Time to analyse

OK, you've now, by wide, general reading, collected lots of information on the topic. It's time to sort through your notes and ideas and analyse them to decide what's relevant and what isn't. Once again, you'll need to apply your critical thinking. At university, it's not enough just to reproduce facts. You need to build an argument and support it with evidence. So, once you've discarded what's irrelevant, you'll have to organise the rest into different approaches, viewpoints, arguments and counter-arguments. The underlying aim is to present a tight, well-argued, well-supported case for your own viewpoint.

By the way, when we say 'discard', we don't mean throw it away. The material may not be relevant in this particular instance but the topic may come up again in a different form and the 'discarded' material may then be relevant. So never throw away notes – apart from anything else, they're all valuable when you're revising for an exam.

Wider considerations

Use a wide range of sources. Don't rely on handouts and notes from a single textbook. You'll get credit for showing that you've looked further afield and found material outside the recommended reading.

When you did your time management plan for the assignment, one of the suggested areas was time allocated for reading. It's all too easy to use 'Oh, I need to do more reading' as an excuse not to start the actual writing. So, when you allocate reading time, make it realistic. Give yourself plenty of time but then stick to it and make yourself move on to the next phase.

Keep a record of what you read. There'll probably be times when you know you read something somewhere that's relevant to the topic you're researching but you can't remember what or where it was. When you make notes, part of your routine should be to include in them the page number, chapter, title, author, publisher and place of publication. You'll be able to find them more quickly and citation and referencing will be much easier.

What next?

Look through our list of instruction words ...

... and decide which ones are asking you to do, describe, analyse or argue. Now do the same thing with some or all of the assignment titles you've been set or ones from past exam papers. In each case, decide which of the four types of approach is needed. Sometimes you may have to do more than one in the same question. For example, you may have to describe something before you can analyse it.

brilliant recap

- Before you start, make sure you understand what's needed.
- Know the common instruction words.
- Manage your time in order to work more efficiently and avoid unnecessary stress.
- Break down the task into its separate elements to make sure you answer the question that's set.
- Find, record and use the resources you'll need to tackle the subject.

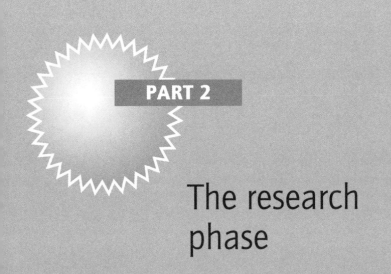

PART 2

The research phase

CHAPTER 4

Learning how to read

Whatever you're studying, it's sure to involve lots of reading. There may be bits you can skim through and there'll definitely be bits you need to linger over to deepen your knowledge and understanding of topics. In this chapter we'll look at some skills which will help you to read more efficiently.

Reading and understanding

Most of the books and chapters you'll be reading as part of your studies will be written in a fairly formal, traditional academic style. Sometimes that can mean they look and feel like heavygoing. Big, unfamiliar words, long sentences, an apparent lack of passion – all these things can make reading seem like hard work. But these materials have been written by people who want to communicate information and/or a point of view, so they're carefully organised to make their points. If you learn how text is structured, you can use that knowledge to help you read it in a way that'll make it understandable and yet save you time. That's what we mean by reading more efficiently.

---

brilliant tip

Most of the time when you're reading for study, you'll be taking notes. It's possible to do both at the same time, but that may not work well because your notes could end up just being a rewrite of the text. If you scan the relevant section of text first, it'll give you a clearer idea of its content and how it fits into the argument. Then you'll be able to write more meaningful (and probably much shorter) notes.

The overall organisation of the text

You'll be dealing with different sorts of texts. They may be recommended by tutors or they may be books and articles you find for yourself when you're expanding your lecture notes or revising. Whatever the source material, the best strategy is to do a quick survey (not a read) to get an overall idea of what's in it. There are various ways of doing this.

- Does the title sound as though it'll be about the things you're looking for?
- Is the author a well-known authority on the subject?
- Does the 'blurb' on the cover confirm that it's relevant to your needs?
- When was the book published? Will you get up-to-date information from it?
- Look at the list of contents. Do they cover the topic areas you need? Are the chapter titles very general or quite detailed?
- Is there a comprehensive index and is it easy to use? Take a quick look for specific references to the material you want.
- And finally, what does the text look like? Is it easy to read and easy to navigate using sub-headings?

These are your starting points. Once you've worked through this list you'll have a better idea of whether that particular piece is valuable for you. It may be that you decide you need to read the whole book, or there may just be certain chapters or pages that cover what you're looking for. Equally, you may decide that there's nothing there which you need at present.

Why are you reading?

This may seem a strange question but it's part of what you need to do to help focus your reading. Before you start the actual reading, make up your mind exactly what it is you're looking for and adapt your approach accordingly.

brilliant tip

- Are you looking for a specific point of information? If so, use chapter titles, subheadings or the index as a guide and only read the relevant pages. It'll speed up the whole process.

- Is the idea to expand your lecture notes by using a textbook? If so, you'll read in a different way, perhaps using points from the lecture to direct your attention. You might also be taking notes which, again, will alter your reading technique.

- Are you reading in order to appreciate the author's style or perhaps the aesthetics of a poem or a work of fiction? If so, you'll read more slowly, taking time to reflect on the choice of words and expressions, and you may reread certain parts.

The structures of academic writing

Academic texts usually follow the same basic pattern. Each part of the argument, as well as the overall piece, consists of an introduction, the main body of the text and a conclusion.

Both the introduction and the conclusion may consist of one paragraph or several. Each paragraph, including those in the main body of the text, has its own particular point to make or develop and each starts with what's called a topic sentence which indicates what the paragraph contains.

brilliant example

The typical layout for a piece of work consisting of five paragraphs looks like this:

- Introduction – topic paragraph.
- Main body – paragraphs 2, 3 and 4, each beginning with a topic sentence.
- Conclusion – terminator paragraph.

The way these paragraphs and the sentences within them fit into the overall argument is usually signalled by 'signpost words'. They guide the reader through the logical structure of the text. For example, the word 'however' warns you to expect that whatever follows it will contrast or conflict with whatever went before it, and if you see 'thus', you'll know that you're about to read a consequence of what went before because it means 'as a result of this'. So look out for signpost words; they'll help you to identify general meanings, changes of direction and the underlying argument.

A quick way of getting a general overview of the text is to read topic and terminator paragraphs, or even just their topic sentences. Unfortunately, that won't be sufficient to supply your needs, but it'll get you focused on what you're likely to gain from your reading of the whole piece.

Another technique is to scan quickly through the text for key words related to your interest. You may notice that several occur in particular paragraphs, which suggests that those paragraphs are worth reading in detail. If there are headings and sub-headings, they'll be very helpful in the same way.

brilliant tip

We're looking at the structures of texts in order to help you to decode them as a reader. It's as well to remember that, if you want to make your own work easier to decode (by a marker, for example), you should use the same layouts and techniques. For both reader and writer, the better the material is structured, the more effective it is at conveying information.

The structural elements in practice

Here's a more detailed example of a piece of writing, with the structural features we've been discussing highlighted for you. We've put the topic sentences in italics and the signpost words in bold.

brilliant example

Introduction, or topic paragraph

Technological advances and skilful marketing have meant that the mobile phone has moved from being simply an accessory to a status as an essential piece of equipment. From teenagers to grandmothers, the nation has taken to the mobile phone as a constant link for business and social purposes. As a phenomenon, the ascendency of the mobile phone, in a multitude of ways, has had a critical impact on the way people organise their lives.

Body text

Clearly, the convenience of the mobile is attractive. It is constantly available to receive or send calls. While these are not cheap, the less expensive text-message alternative provides a similar 'constant contact' facility. At a personal and social level, this brings peace of mind to parents because teenagers can locate them and be located by them at the press of a button. **However,** in business terms, while it means that employees are constantly accessible and, with more sophisticated models, can also access internet communications, there is no escape from the workplace.

The emergence of abbreviated text-message language has wrought a change in everyday print. **For example**, pupils and students have been known to submit written work using text-message symbols and language. Some have declared this to mark the demise of standard English. **Furthermore,** the accessibility of the mobile phone has become a problem in colleges and universities where it has been known for students in examinations to use the texting facility to obtain information required.

The ubiquity of the mobile phone has generated changes in the way that services are offered. **For instance**, this means that trains, buses, and restaurants have declared 'silent zones' where the mobile is not permitted in order to give others a rest from the 'I'm on the train' style mobile phone conversation.

*While the marked increase in mobile phone sales indicates that many in the population have embraced this technology, **by contrast**,* 'mobile' culture has not been without its critics. Real concerns have been expressed about the potential dangers that can be encountered through mobile phone use.

One such danger is that associated with driving while speaking on a mobile. A body of case law has been accumulated to support the introduction of new legislation outlawing the use of hand-held mobile phones by drivers while driving. The enforcement of this legislation is virtually impossible to police and, **thus,** much is down to the commonsense and responsibility of drivers. **Again,** technology has risen to meet the contingency with the development of 'hands-free' phones which can be used while driving and without infringing the law.

A further danger is an unseen one, namely, the impact of the radiation from mobile phones on the human brain. Research is not well advanced in this area and data related to specific absorption rates (SARs) from the use of mobile phones and its effect on brain tissue is not yet available for evaluation. **Nevertheless**, although this lack of evidence is acknowledged by mobile phone companies, they advise that hands-free devices reduce the SARs levels by 98%.

Mobile phone controversy is not confined only to the potential dangers related to the units alone; some people have serious concerns about the impact mobile phone masts have on the area surrounding them. The fear is that radiation from masts could induce serious illness among those living near such masts. **While** evidence refuting or supporting this view remains inconclusive, there appears to be much more justification for concern about emissions from television transmitters and national grid pylons which emit far higher levels of electro-magnetic radiation. **Yet**, little correlation appears to have been made between this fundamental of electrical engineering and the technology of telecommunications.

Conclusion, or terminator paragraph

In summary, although it appears that there are enormous benefits to mobile phone users, it is clear that there are many unanswered questions about the impact of their use on individuals. At one level, these represent an intrusion on personal privacy whether as a user or as a bystander obliged to listen to multiple one-sided conversations in public places. **More significantly**, there is the potential for unseen damage to the health of individual users as they clamp their mobiles to their ears. **Whereas** the individual has a choice to use or not to use a mobile phone, people have fewer choices in relation to exposure to dangerous emissions from masts. **While** the output from phone masts is worthy of further investigation, it is in the more general context of emissions from electro-magnetic masts of all types that serious research needs to be developed.

Speed-reading

The basic techniques of speed-reading were developed in the 1950s by Evelyn Wood, an American educator. She set up institutes to teach students skills which enabled them to read hundreds of words a minute. Her methods have been used in many fields where busy people need to read and understand lengthy papers as quickly as possible.

The techniques

People who read quickly don't read each word as a separate unit. They use their peripheral vision which, if you stare straight ahead, is what you see at the edges of your vision to the right and the left. By doing this, they take in groups of words at a time. So, instead of reading:

Students need to read many books in the course of studying

they read:

(Students need) (to read many books) (in the course of) (studying)

In other words, rather than moving their eyes eleven times, once for each word, they move them four times. It's obviously a more efficient and less tiring way of reading. Studies have also shown that people who read slowly are less likely to gather information quickly enough for the brain to understand it, so reading slowly may actually make comprehension more difficult.

Before we go any further, maybe you'd like to check your own reading speed. (Although not if you're just using it as a displacement activity!) There are two possible methods: one measures how much you can read in a given time, the other how long it takes you to read a specified amount of text.

In Method A you'll read for a particular length of time.

- Choose a chapter from a textbook. Don't use a newspaper or journal because the text there is often printed in columns.

- Calculate the average number of words to a line – e.g. if there are 50 words in five lines, that's ten words per line.

- Now count the number of lines per page. Let's say it's 41.

- Multiply the number of words per line by the number of pages – that's 10 x 41 = 410 words on each page.

- Start at the beginning of your chosen text and read for a set period of time – let's say four minutes – without stopping. Note the point on the page at which the time runs out.

- Let's assume that you managed two and a half pages in four minutes. To find out how many words that is, multiply 410 (the number of words per page) by 2.5 (the number of pages you read). That gives you 1025 total words read.

- Now divide that by four (the number of minutes you read) and it shows that you've averaged 256 words per minute (wpm).

Method B uses a text of a known length.

- Choose a text and count the number of words in it. Let's say it's 744.

- Time how long you take to read it. We'll say 170 seconds.

- To find how many minutes that is in decimal form, divide it by 60, which gives you 2.8.

- Now divide the total words by 2.8 and you get a reading speed of 266 wpm.

Since you're a student and you do quite a bit of reading, you probably already use a version of fast reading to some extent but there are ways of improving your technique.

Eye gymnastics

Here's an exercise which helps to train your eyes to use your peripheral vision when you're reading. As you do it, your eyes will be forced to jump from one group of words to the next, focusing on the centre each time. Try to read the text quite quickly from left to right in the normal way. If you feel some discomfort behind your eyes, it means they're adjusting to this new way of moving. Just keep practising. You can use this text as a piece of training equipment just as you'd use a treadmill or a barbell.

Learning to read quickly is a skill you must develop.
If you have to read a new piece of text you'll find it useful
first of all to read the first paragraph
then the last of the section, chapter or article.
From this you should be able to gauge
the context and general outline of the topic
under discussion. While it is true that all academic texts
should have been well edited before publication,
it does not follow that every text conforms to
these conventions. However, a well-written
academic text should follow this pattern
and, as a reader, you should exploit this convention
to help you understand the overall context
before you embark on intensive reading of the text.

When you start taking notes you should not begin
by sitting with notepad ready and pen poised.
Certainly make a note of publication details
for your bibliography, but don't try to start taking notes
at the same time as beginning your first reading.
It is better to read first, reflect, recall
and then write notes based on what you remember.

This gives you	a framework	around which
you should	organise your notes	after you have read
the text intensively.	People who start	by writing notes
as soon as	they open the book	will end up
copying	more and more	as they get
more tired.	In this case	very little
reflection or learning	is achieved.	

Finger-tracing

Another technique is finger-tracing. As its name suggests, it's when you run your finger along under the line of text you're reading. It follows the path of your eyes across the page, starting and stopping a word or two from either side. This keeps your mind focused on what you're actually reading and stops you skipping back to previous sentences or jumping forward to the text that follows, and it helps to increase your eye speed. Some people use a bookmark or ruler held just under the line they're reading; it's a useful guide and works in the same way.

Try this exercise:

- Choose a reading passage about two pages long. Note your starting and finishing time and calculate your reading speed using Method B.

- Take a break of 40–60 minutes then go back to the text and run your finger along the lines much faster than you could possibly read it.

- Now do the same thing again but slowly enough for you to be just able to read it. Note how long it takes you this time and work out your wpm again. You'll probably find that you're faster this time round.

- Now do the same exercise at the same time of day over a week, using texts of the same sort of length and complexity.

Speeding up and slowing down

The average reading speed is around 265 wpm but various factors may make that slightly slower for university students. Texts may be more difficult, their terminology unfamiliar, and they may be discussing quite complex concepts which need to be absorbed. All these things can slow down a reading. But the more familiar you become with your subjects and the issues being covered in your course, the faster you'll be able to read.

As well as trying to get faster, you should think too about things which might slow you down. They could include:

- distractions such as background noise, TV, music, talking
- sounding each word as you read it aloud
- reading word by word
- being over-tired
- poor eyesight – your eyes are too important to neglect, so get them tested; reading glasses can make a big difference to your studying comfort as well as to your speed reading
- poor lighting – if you can, read using a lamp that can shine directly onto the text; reading in poor light causes eye strain, which makes it harder to concentrate and cuts down your reading time.

Other strategies

- **Skimming**. Let your eye run quickly down a list or over a page looking for a key word or phrase, just as you do when looking for a name in a phone book. That's the way to find a specific piece of information you're looking for.
- **Scanning**. Let your eye run quickly over a chapter this time. It'll give you an idea of what the chapter's about before you start.
- **Picking out the topic sentences**. Read the topic sentences to add more detail to the overview you got from scanning.

It'll help you to understand what's being conveyed before you study-read the whole text.

- **Identifying the signpost words**. They'll guide you through the logical process mapped out by the author.

- **Recognising clusters of words which go together grammatically**. As you read, group words in clusters according to their natural sense. It's what you did in the eye gymnastics exercise and it'll help you to make fewer eye movements.

- **Taking cues from punctuation**. Full stops, commas and other punctuation marks are valuable clues when it comes to understanding a text. They separate chunks of meaning, indicate points to emphasise, mark transition points and help comprehension in many other ways. As both reader and writer, you should never underestimate the importance of punctuation.

Speed with comprehension

Measuring speed on its own gives a false result. It's all very well having a wpm of 300 plus but, if you don't understand what you're reading, you're wasting your time. So speed reading needs to be matched by a good level of comprehension. There are ways of testing your understanding to make sure you've grasped the main points of what you've been reading. The one we'll look at is called the SQ3R method, which stands for Survey, Question, Read, Recall and Review. It's also useful when you're revising for exams because it helps to develop memory and learning skills simultaneously.

With the SQ3R method, you can't just read on autopilot and not retain much, you have to process the material as you go along. Let's go through the five stages: S, Q, R, R, R.

Survey

- Read the first paragraph (topic paragraph) and last paragraph (terminator paragraph) of a chapter or page of notes.
- Read the topic sentences of all the paragraphs between them.
- If there are headings and sub-headings, focus on them.
- Study graphs and diagrams for important features.

Question

- What do you already know about this topic?
- What's the author likely to tell you?
- What specifically do you need to find out?

Read

- Read the entire section quickly to get the gist of it, using finger-tracing if it helps.
- Go back to the question stage. Check and revise if necessary the answers you gave then.
- Look for key words, key statements, signpost words.
- Don't stop to look up unknown words – get it read.

Recall

- Turn the book or your notes over and try to remember as much as possible.
- Make important pattern headings/notes/diagrams/flow charts.
- Look at the text again and see how accurate your recall was. Do this after every 20 minutes of reading.

Review

- Take a break, then try to recall the main points.

Reading effectively and with understanding

After everything we've said, it must be obvious that reading isn't the simple process that most people assume it to be. You need strategies and practice to make it work for you. So start by thinking about why you're reading. Look at the material you've already collected on the subject, such as lecture notes, which can remind you of how a topic was presented, what arguments were used or how a procedure was followed. Decide whether you're trying to get a general overview or identify additional specific information.

Once you've decided that, use a technique and material that suits your needs and a reading speed that fits the type of text you've chosen. For example, an interesting article in a newspaper won't demand much in the way of intensive reading, whereas an important chapter in an academic book will.

Get the general message before focusing on the difficult bits. Not all texts are reader-friendly. If you come across a section of text that's difficult to understand, skip over it. Forcing yourself to read and reread it won't make it any clearer. Read on and then, when you come to a natural break in the text – the end of a chapter or section – go back to the hard bit and try again. It'll probably make more sense now because you've got a better feel for the context. The same advice applies to new or difficult words. Don't stop every time you come across one; read on and try to get an idea of what it might mean from the rest of the text. You can look it up when you've finished and add it to your personal glossary.

Follow up references in your text. Be aware of any citations to other authors you find there. They won't all be relevant to the aim of your reading, but it's worth making a quick note of any that look interesting as you come across them. You'll usually find the full publication details at the end of the chapter, article or book, and you can use them to find and read them when you've finished the current text.

> ### ⭐ brilliant tip
>
> Take regular breaks. If you try to read continuously over a long period of time you'll retain less. You can concentrate well for 20 minutes and more but, after 40 minutes, the mind begins to wander. Take plenty of rests (but make sure they don't start getting longer than the actual studying periods).

What next?

Check your reading speed ...

... using the two methods we've described. If you think it's slow, try out some of the techniques and exercises we've outlined. Decide which ones suit you, use them for a while, then check to see if your speed's improved.

Practise surveying a text ...

... using a book from your reading list. Rather than simply opening it at a particular page, spend five or ten minutes surveying the whole book. Think about how the author has organised the content and why. Remember this as you read the text, and reflect on whether it's helped you to understand and absorb the content more easily.

Remember that ...

... grammar, punctuation and spelling provide useful clues to meaning. Look for these visual cues and use them to help both your speed and comprehension.

brilliant recap

- Survey a text's overall organisation to get a general idea of its contents and potential usefulness for your project.

- Make sure your writing is structured at the level of the entire text and that your paragraphs and sentences help to create and sustain that structure.

- Practise and develop your own speed-reading techniques.

- Always strive to achieve a balance between reading the text quickly and understanding it.

CHAPTER 5

Libraries: more than just books

Naturally enough, when you're preparing an essay or an assignment you'll be expected to look at the relevant books on your reading list. But they're just part of the written word resources you'll need. At university, you're independent and have to take responsibility for your own choices. So you'll also be expected to locate additional material for yourself, which means developing the skills to recognise where the gaps in your reading are and how to plug them. What we're talking about is information literacy.

How to use the library

You might be thinking this is an unnecessary chapter. After all, we all know what libraries are and what you do in them. You go there, borrow a book, and that's it. Maybe – but university libraries are much more than collections of books and journals. For students, they're a major resource with information in many forms. As well as the items they carry on their shelves, they represent electronic gateways to a massive amount of online information. With so much material at your fingertips and such specific topics to research, you need to know how to focus on what's available, what's relevant and how to access it in its most useful forms.

More than books

As well as books, most university libraries also have copies of some newspapers, periodicals and academic journals. There'll be many kinds of reference materials, perhaps slides, photographs, videos and DVDs. There'll also be areas set aside for particular types of study. The most obvious are the quiet study areas but there may also be places for group work where you're allowed to discuss things. Photocopiers and printers will probably be available, along with computing terminals and possibly a wireless network. You'll have access to online catalogues and, of course, the library staff are there to support you, either in person or through the library website. So there's definitely more than books.

brilliant tip

Some reading lists are long and the books on them are expensive. If you need to refer to a particular book frequently and/or it relates closely to your lectures and coursework, it's obviously worth buying your own copy. But if not, check to see if it's in the library and how many copies they carry. (You may have problems if all the other students in your class need to consult the same book at the same time.)

E-resources

Today, vast amounts of material are accessible online in just about every area of interest. Libraries have subscriptions to e-book repositories, e-journals, e-newspapers and online dictionaries and encyclopaedias. Your institution will have its own dedicated system of access to these digitised and web-based resources and you'll probably need a password. It'll pay you to get to know the details of your system as early as possible.

Some e-book facilities, such as ebrary, have extra tools that let you search, make notes and consult linked online dictionaries to check the meanings of words.

There are now many electronic databases that make it easier to get access to information from public bodies, and most of them are available online. For example, you can look at statistical population details on the National Statistics website (www.statistics.gov.uk), and any papers and publications produced by the Houses of Parliament at www.parliament.uk. Access to academic journals and other material will depend whether your library subscribes to them or not, so find out which search engines and databases are available to you.

Paper-based resources

The most obvious of these are the books.

- Your prescribed texts link with the content of your course.
- General textbooks provide a broader overview of the subject.
- Supplementary texts discuss topics in greater depth.

Then come the many different kinds of reference books.

- Standard dictionaries help with spelling, pronunciation and meaning.
- Bilingual dictionaries translate words and expressions in two languages.
- Subject-specific dictionaries define important terms relating to a particular discipline.
- General encyclopaedias provide a quick overview of or introduction to a new topic.
- Discipline-specific encyclopaedias have in-depth coverage of specific topics.
- Biographical dictionaries and other material are excellent sources of information on both contemporary and historical figures.

- Yearbooks and directories carry up-to-date information on organisations.

- Atlases provide geographical and historical information.

Finally, there are newspapers and journals.

- Newspapers, both daily and weekly, cover contemporary issues.

- Periodicals and academic journals are publications which are specific to a particular discipline or subject. They usually appear three or four times a year and provide new ideas, reports and comment on current research issues.

- Popular periodicals, such as *Nature, New Scientist* and *The Economist*, deal with broader issues and emerging trends in the fields of study indicated by their titles.

Shared library resources

Many university libraries share resources with those of neighbouring institutions. They're all linked to the British Library too, which is the national library of the UK. This receives a copy of every publication produced in the UK and Ireland, and its massive collection of over 150 million items increases by 3 million every year. Some university libraries are known as European Documentation Centres (http://europa.eu/europedirect/meet_us/interactive_map/index_en.htm). They hold important documents of the European Union.

Getting to know the system

You'll have plenty to be thinking about without having to worry whether books are on the shelves, overdue, on short or long term loans and all the rest of it, so find out the rules you need to know as a borrower.

⚡ brilliant questions and answers

Q How many books can I borrow at any one time?

A That depends on your status. Staff and postgraduate students can usually borrow more books than undergraduates.

Q How long can I keep the item I've borrowed?

A It depends on what it is. Normal loans are usually for several weeks. But there may be a big demand for some books because they're prescribed texts, so they may be put on a short-loan system. That means you can take them out but have to hand them back earlier than with 'normal' books – maybe in a matter of a few hours, but usually it's a few days.

Q What's the fine if I keep it longer than I'm supposed to?

A It depends on the sort of book. If it's a short-term loan, the fine will be higher than 'normal' loans. It may just be a few pence but think about it. If you've got 10 books you should have handed back two weeks ago, that'll cost you £10 or more.

Q How can I renew the loan?

A By phone with most libraries and – more and more – online. Check your university's home page.

Electronic book tagging

Most universities operate a system of electronic 'book tagging' to make sure that resources can't be taken out without being logged out to a particular user. This means that all books need to be 'de-activated' before you can take them outside the library.

Regulations and codes of conduct

You'll see notices on leaflets and websites telling or remind-ing you of the library rules. They're important because they're there to protect the resources and also to regulate the studying environment for you and all the other users, asking you to be aware of the needs of those studying around you. In particular, they spell out your legal responsibilities under copyright law and tell you how much you can photocopy from a specific book or document.

Important library skills

Whatever you're writing, you'll need information either to supplement what you already know or to acquire new knowledge. To do that, you'll have to master some basic skills.

- You'll need to be familiar with how electronic catalogues work to avoid wasting time in fruitless searches. Most let you search by author, title or subject, but there may be other alternatives on your system.

- When you identify the book that you want from the catalogue, you'll want to know which shelf it's on. So you need to take a note of two things: the location (because the book might even be in another site library) and the number, which may be a sequence of letters and/or numbers depending on the system your library uses. It's on the spine of the book and books are all arranged in sequence in stacks. At the end of each stack you'll find the numbers of the first and last books in the sequence they contain. If you can't find what you're looking for, library staff will help you.

- Sometimes a book may not be available in your own library and you may want to borrow it from another UK library. There's usually a librarian who's responsible for inter-library loans so that's the person you need to consult. Be careful, though, there's usually a fee to pay for this and you're the one who has to pay it.

- We spoke earlier of the various e-resources you might use. Normally, you'll access them through the library's website.

Some are open-access but for others you'll need a password so that publishers can check that your library has subscribed to a particular resource and that you have access rights. Systems vary but usually there'll be special training sessions in lectures or arranged independently in the library. There's a wealth of material; don't be fazed by it. Ask a librarian to help you find your way around it all.

brilliant tip

Imagine your lecturer has mentioned an article by someone called Nichol which you should read. You look up the name but there's no sign of the article. That may be because she may be called Nicol, Nicoll, Nickol or many other variations of the surname. So, if you haven't seen a name written down (in your course handbook, for example), try different options to get the one you want.

Look further afield

Find and join the local public library. It may have some texts relevant to your course and they won't be in such heavy demand as those in the university library. Some university libraries have agreements with other similar ones in the area, including national libraries. This obviously extends the resources available to you and you should take advantage of such arrangements. You can use the facilities and sometimes even borrow books from partner libraries.

Check out what these other libraries are like, too. You may find some with different study areas that are more convenient or that suit your moods, learning preference or personality. On the other hand, you may prefer peace and quiet or work better if there's some activity around you as you study.

And make sure you know about all the alternative library facilities on your campus. There may be satellite libraries on different parts of the site or in different buildings. Some of these may be departmental libraries with specialist resources. They may also hold duplicates of books in the main library.

Of course, finding information on the shelves and online is only the first step. It's important to know how best to use it for your studies. Next you need to evaluate it and use it appropriately in your note-making and academic writing. The reason we mention this here is that it helps enormously if, when you find the information you need, you note the details of where you found it. We'll deal with how to do that later but it's never too early to point out that plagiarism is theft. So, if you use material from a specific book, article or other publication, always acknowledge where it came from and who wrote it.

brilliant examples

There are two main cataloguing systems; the one your library uses will be explained in leaflets or during the library tour.

The two systems are:

- The Dewey decimal system, in which each book is given a number. For example, editions of Shakespeare's *Hamlet* are filed under 822.33.
- The Library of Congress system, which uses an alphanumeric code, so the same editions of *Hamlet* would be filed under PR2807.

There may be small variations in how these are interpreted, so the important thing is to find out exactly how your own library's system works.

What next?

Try to go on a library tour ...

... and if you see or hear things you don't understand, ask about them. In many ways university libraries are different from public libraries and they've got much more to offer. If your university doesn't organise tours, see if you can take a virtual tour using your university library's website.

Get to know the electronic library resources ...

... particularly any which are specific to your own subjects, and explore the shelves covering your subject area. Find this area by looking in the library catalogue and the information on the book stacks. When you do, browse through what's there. You may find interesting books and catalogues which you might not have come across otherwise.

brilliant recap

- Libraries are most than just books. Discover the many facilities and resources available.
- Find out how the library system works – administrative procedures, borrowing books, using catalogues and e-resources, finding your way around.
- Expand your access to resources by joining other libraries.

CHAPTER 6

Turning reading into notes

Most courses provide recommended reading lists. They'll probably include textbooks, journal articles and web-based materials. Sometimes you'll get specific references to topics covered in these texts but at other times it'll be up to you to find the relevant material for yourself. When you do, you'll want to make a note of it in a form that's easy to create and just as easy to find and understand when you have an essay to write or want to revise for exams. In this chapter, we'll look at both general and specific aspects of making notes.

The need for notes

With lectures, tutorials and your own reading bombarding you with information, there's just too much of it for you to retain. So you need either ways to compress it or maps which take you to the particular topic you're looking for. Notes fulfil both these functions.

brilliant tip

Develop good habits and you'll save lots of time both with making notes and consulting them later. So right from the start, remember two techniques:

● Before you do anything else, make a note of the full details of the source. That means the author's name and initials, the title, the publisher and the date and place it was published. Don't forget to add the chapter and pages these particular notes refer to. This is crucial if you're going to be quoting any of it in your written work.

● Make your notes personal by using underlining, highlighting, colour coding, numbered lists, bullet points, mnemonics or anything else which helps you to find your way around them. Choose a distinctive layout, perhaps using boxes for important points. If you're consistent with this, it'll make the different aspects of your notes instantly recognisable.

What should be in them?

When you're writing an assignment, you'll probably be looking for information from a variety of sources. In some of them, you'll just be selecting single isolated points; in others your reading will be more intensive. So the first thing for you to decide is why you're actually making the notes. There are many possible reasons. You may want to:

● create an overview of the subject

● record a sequence or process

● analyse a problem

● isolate the logical steps of an argument

- compare different viewpoints
- borrow quotes to support a point you're making
- add your own ideas to the text or comment on the points it's making
- link something in the text with points that have cropped up in a lecture or tutorial.

As you can see, these reasons can be very varied and their style, detail and depth will alter according to their purpose.

The majority of people probably start with a sheet of paper in front of them and a pen clutched in their hand. They open the book, start reading and begin jotting down 'important' points as they go along. If you're one of these, the problem is that you end up writing out whole chunks of the text and it doesn't encourage you to think much about what you're reading; it goes from the page to your notebook without dwelling long in your head. So, instead, once you've decided why you're making notes, get used to following a routine.

- Look at your assignment again and decide what you need.
- Scan the section you'll be reading.
- Establish what the writer's trying to do. Is it a narrative of events or a process, a statement of facts, an explanation, a presentation of a logical argument, an analysis of a problem, a critique of an argument?
- Work out the writer's approach and viewpoint and decide how it relates to what you're looking for.
- Decide what style and layout are best for that particular task.

Finally, don't just copy the author's words, use your own. It's his meaning you want, not his words. But if you do want to copy something directly from the text, put it in quote marks and note carefully the page on which you found it.

Note-making formats

When you think about making notes, it's perhaps automatic to assume that you start on line one and add notes as you work down the page. This is fine, but there are different formats for different purposes. If you wanted, for example, to stress the two sides of a particular argument, it might be more helpful to have two columns side by side, one carrying points for, the other points against. Or if you were brainstorming and just jotting down disparate ideas, they wouldn't necessarily follow a connected, linear sequence. In that case, it might make sense to use what's called a mind map or spider diagram, where you write ideas and concepts down as they occur, placing ideas and concepts near ones which are similar or in a separate area and using lines to connect notes that may belong together.

In fact, we can identify seven basic note-making formats, although there are variations on all of them.

Key word notes

This is a fairly obvious and common format. You identify each topic by a key word which you jot down on the left, maybe in the margin. Then you write all the points relating to that topic opposite it. It means that you can quickly find a specific part of the argument and all its aspects are gathered conveniently together. But this does depend on the source text having a systematic structure. If it doesn't, you may find you've moved on to other topics and then there's a reference back to a previous one, so you have to jump back in your notes – as a result, you might lose the thread of your reading, there may not be enough space left on the page, and so on.

Linear notes

Another obvious format. Once again, it helps if the text is presented logically. This time, instead of key words, you use numbers. But not just 1, 2, 3 and so on. Think of 1 as a keyword and 1.1, 1.2, 1.3, 1.4 as the various points relating to it. Again, it's a good way to gather and organise material but, as before, if you come across something that you want to add under an earlier number, it may be hard to find room for it in the sequence.

Timelines

This has limited use as a format. It consists of setting a timeline on the left and noting events or the stages in a process opposite the appropriate times and/or dates. Once again, it's difficult to go back and insert material at an earlier time. On the other hand, it does give a strong visual aid if the reason for making the notes is to help you remember sequences.

Flowcharts

This is another way of making a relatively simple visual representation of what may be a complex process. You might, for example, be reading about the development of a piece of equipment from its original conception (and the conditions in which it was conceived) to its production. A flowchart would allow you to break the whole process down into, for example, preliminary discussions, research phase, various forms of testing, final trials, production, operational application. Arrows leading from one phase to the next would trace a clear path through the process. It's a format that's useful in specific circumstances but it does need a lot of space and it may also have circuitous little flows weaving around the main one.

Concept maps/mind maps

In a way, these are a sort of 'crash-bang-wallop' style of note-making. The paper is usually set in landscape rather than the usual portrait format and ideas, concepts and statements are spread all over it with lines connecting those which might be linked together in terms of meaning or impact. The advantage is that they hold all the information on a single page, but they can get very messy as the information multiplies and there are sometimes so many points and lines that they're hard to follow.

Matrix notes/grid notes

Creating a table or matrix is obviously useful if your notes are recording different viewpoints, approaches, applications. It would, for example, be perfect if you were dealing with a problem that consisted of different elements and involved several contrasting viewpoints on those elements. An article on traffic problems might have separate columns for the views of the government, the police, local businesses, the local community. The various rows in the grid could then be labelled to test their attitudes to pedestrianisation, parking fees and fines, congestion charges, commercial access, car-sharing schemes. It gives a quick, easy-to-use overview of the issues and how they combine or contrast but doesn't allow much space to develop notes or add extra information.

Herringbone maps

This may sound a strange label but it's the perfect image for a format that lets you lay out opposing sides of an argument. Imagine the usual cartoon version of a fishbone, with a spine down the middle and bones sticking out on either side. On one side, the 'bones' carry statements for an argument, on the other are the statements against. It's simple and effective. But it's also limited. There's no obvious place for statements that are ambiguous or refer to things other than the arguments for and against. And you might find you need a very long herring as you read more and more of the text and make more and more notes.

Getting personal

We keep referring to books, articles and online sites as resources, but the same word applies to your notes. Never throw them away; you've spent lots of time collecting them and they're excellent when it comes to revising. In fact, you may well find that, by the time you get to the exams, they'll refresh your memory of the subject and even make it clearer than it was when you were writing them. They've distilled its essence and stripped away any confusions there might have been on the first read of the text.

brilliant tip

Don't try to cram too much information onto a sheet. Leave white space around lists or other important items of information. It'll not only help you to view and remember the information more easily but also leave space for any extra details you might want to add later.

The visual aspects of your notes are important. They should be memorable and recognisable. Be careful, though – don't turn the business of making them look good into a displacement activity. The idea isn't to make them look pretty or create some sort of art form out of them, it's to create patterns, colours and shapes that trigger your recall.

Find ways of abbreviating what you write. Use familiar abbreviations such as NATO or DNA and the common ones like e.g., i.e., etc., but develop your own shorthand, too. You could use maths symbols, text-messaging techniques, or words from other languages. When we started writing this book, the phrase 'essay or assignment' was occurring quite frequently (naturally enough) so we used the Tools > AutoCorrect function to represent it with a single key – the hash sign. You can do the same thing with a pen – writing one little symbol instead of ten letters saves ages.

You can also save time by photocopying relevant pages. This is useful if you don't need many notes on a topic or maybe when there's a lot of demand for a particular book and it's on short loan in the library. It's easier to get a photocopy and high-light the key bits or add your notes in the margins. In this case, though, it's important to remember that copyright law means that there are restrictions on photocopying. Check what they are by looking at notices in your library.

If you copy down a direct quotation from the text, make sure you note the page number. When you then use it in your assignment, write the name of the author, date of publication and page number beside the quotation. We'll go into this in more detail later in the book.

What next?

Look for a general dictionary ...

... that gives a comprehensive list of abbreviations and see which ones might be useful for you. Also, check a subject-specific dictionary for lists of specialist abbreviations. You'll not only be able to use them yourself but you'll know where to look if you come across one that's unfamiliar as you're reading.

Everyone has a different method ...

... of note-making and we've actually suggested that you should personalise yours to suit your style. So compare your notes with those of a classmate, on the same piece of text if possible. Talk about what you've chosen to note and why; it'll help both of you to appreciate any differences in reasoning, understanding, logic.

Don't hesitate to try different styles ...

... A strategy that works well for some things may be less good for others. Also, as you progress, the sorts of books you read may change and call for different approaches. So find a style that suits you but always be open to new things. Stay flexible.

 brilliant recap

- Ask yourself why you're taking the notes and what should be in them.
- Understand the different ways of taking notes and try different formats for different exercises.
- Personalise your note-making to help you find what you're looking for when you need it for essays and/or exams.

CHAPTER 7

The importance of critical thinking

The ability to think critically is probably the most valuable skill you'll develop at university. It's an ability with uses and applications in all walks of work and life. So we need to do some thinking about thinking.

A logical approach to analysis, synthesis and problem-solving

Is it actually possible to think better? Are there theories or techniques that can help? Well, most university teaching is based on the assumption that you can and there are. You won't get good marks simply by having a good memory, recalling facts and churning them out. At university you're expected to analyse and synthesise those facts, reach an opinion about them and support it with evidence and argument. If you're systematic and methodical about doing this, it'll help with all sorts of tasks, from the easy to the more challenging.

brilliant definition

Critical thinking

The first reaction to the words 'critical' and 'criticism' is usually to assume they're negative. But critical thinking is positive. It means considering all aspects of a topic and then making a careful judgement about it. Critical thinking is good, creative thinking.

Thinking about thinking

A famous educational psychologist, Benjamin Bloom, and some of his colleagues listed six steps in learning and thinking in education:

- knowledge
- comprehension
- application
- analysis
- synthesis
- evaluation.

Their analysis was very detailed but for our purposes it's enough to understand what these different phases mean in more general terms. They can be seen as a natural progression. It's probably obvious, for example, that the things you did at school involved mainly knowledge, comprehension and application. At university, you need to do more analysis, synthesis and evaluation. That's easier to understand if you think of the types of exercises you'll be expected to do:

- essay writing in the arts and social sciences
- reports on problem-based learning in medicine and nursing
- case-based scenarios in law
- reports on project-based practical work in the sciences.

All of these call for basic knowledge, understanding and an ability to apply that knowledge and understanding. But they also expect you to look more deeply into ideas and theories, bring different thoughts together and make judgements about the results. In other words, you must be able to analyse, synthesise and evaluate. In subjects such as art and design, architecture, drama or English composition, synthesis might be replaced by creative thinking. But creative thinking is also critical thinking.

In fact, some of the instructions you get for writing assignments and other forms of assessment hint at the sort of thinking the examiner is expecting from you. You're often asked to 'discuss', 'compare', describe', 'analyse' and so on. There's no rule to link any of them with a specific type of thinking but they can guide you.

brilliant definitions

Knowledge

If you know a fact, you can recall or recognise it but you don't necessarily understand it at a higher level. So the words 'define', 'describe', 'identify' and similar expressions are asking you to use knowledge.

Comprehension

Comprehending a fact means that you do understand what it means, which puts you in a position to 'contrast', 'discuss', or 'interpret'.

Application

Knowing and understanding a fact means you know how to use or 'apply' it to 'demonstrate', 'calculate' or 'illustrate'.

Analysis

The next step is being able to break knowledge down into parts and show how they fit together, so you can 'analyse', 'explain' and 'compare'.

Synthesis

Synthesising is the ability to select relevant facts from your knowledge and use them in different ways or different contexts, to create something new. That's what you need to do when asked to 'compose', 'create', or 'integrate'.

Evaluation

After all of that, you're in a position to evaluate facts and information and arrive at a judgement. You can then 'recommend', 'support', and 'draw a conclusion'.

Be careful, though. This isn't a set of fixed 'rules'. For example, if you're asked to 'describe' something in the sciences, you may simply have to note what you observe – Element A was added to Element B and resulted in Reaction X. The same word in architecture, however, might call for much more complex skills and theoretical perspectives.

The 'six steps' in practice

In order to illustrate more clearly the nature of the different phases, let's apply them to three general types of discipline – law, arts subjects, numerical subjects.

Law

- **Knowledge** – you know the name and date of a case, statute or treaty but don't understand its relevance.

- **Comprehension** – you understand both the principle of law in the legislation or case and its wider context.

- **Application** – you're able to identify situations to which the principle would apply.

- **Analysis** – you can see how the facts of a particular scenario relate to the principle and use that knowledge to uncover the extent of its application.

- **Synthesis** – using reasoning and analogy, you can predict how the law might be applied in other circumstances.

- **Evaluation** – you're able to consider the various options and use your judgement as a basis for advising a client.

Arts (e.g. History or Politics)

- **Knowledge** – you know that a river is an important geographical and political boundary in international relations, but you don't know why.

- **Comprehension** – you understand that the river forms a natural barrier, which can be easily identified and defended.

- **Application** – you can use this knowledge to explain the terms of a peace treaty.

- **Analysis** – you can see that the fact that the river is a boundary is important for signatories to the peace treaty in terms of their possible gains or losses of territory.

- **Synthesis** – you can relate this awareness to the recurrence of the same issue in later treaties and its possible implications.

- **Evaluation** – you can discuss whether this boundary was an obstacle to resolving the terms of the treaty to the satisfaction of all parties.

Numerical subjects

- **Knowledge** – you can write down a particular mathematical equation, without understanding what the symbols mean or where it might be applied.

- **Comprehension** – you understand what the symbols mean and how and when to apply the equation

- **Application** – if you have the background information you can use the equation to obtain a result.

- **Analysis** – you can explain the theoretical process involved in deriving the equation.

- **Synthesis** – you can take one equation, link it with another and arrive at a new mathematical relationship or conclusion.

- **Evaluation** – you can discuss the limitations of an equation based on its derivation and the underlying assumptions behind this.

A system for critical thinking

OK, so you have a particular problem and you feel that critical thinking will help you solve it. It could be an essay question, something arising from problem-based learning, or even something as ordinary as deciding what type of car to buy or where to rent a flat. The points discussed below will help you to organise your thinking in a methodical way. They're not in themselves a solution; they're simply stages you might go through to reach a conclusion. Reject them, adapt them, change their order but think about them and get what suits you best from them.

What's the problem?

First of all, you need to be sure that there really is a problem or that it really is what you think it is rather than something else. Write down a description of it and be very precise with your wording. If it's a specific question you've been given, analyse its phrasing carefully, looking for alternative meanings.

How do you approach it?

Try some brainstorming either on your own or with others in a group. That may throw up some possible solutions or viewpoints.

Look at it from all possible angles and write down everything you come up with, even if you're not sure it's relevant or important. If you use a 'spider diagram' or 'mind map' that might help you to make associations and multiply the ideas you're having.

When you're satisfied that you've had a thorough go at exploring lots of ideas, try to arrange them into categories or sub-headings. Alternatively, you could group them as arguments for and against a particular viewpoint.

Once you've got them relatively organised, you can start eliminating the ones that are trivial or irrelevant and sort the rest into some sort of order of priority. This is where you'll be using your analytical skills.

Back up the information with evidence

Now that you've narrowed (or maybe broadened) your focus, make sure you understand the facts. You'll probably need to collect more information and ideas to extend your response, so find some examples or suggest a range of interpretations or approaches which support your viewpoint. You might only need to use dictionaries and technical works to find out the precise meaning of key words; or you might discuss your ideas with your fellow students or a tutor; or you could read a few texts to see what other people have said about the topic.

Assemble your case

You've gathered lots of information, so it's time to make sure it's all relevant and does apply to your question. Look at the question again, check that you really do understand it, and start organising what you've collected. Some of it will support your argument, some of it will oppose it. Maybe a table or grid would help you to get it organised and see the balance you have between for and against. If any of the material is dubious, get rid of it. You want the strongest possible case, with no trivial or irrelevant distractions.

Build to a conclusion

By this stage, you've done so much thinking about it and gathered so much material that you'll probably have formed a strong personal viewpoint. What you have to do now is build your discussion with a view to making that your conclusion. You know what you want to say, so just say it. But be careful. It's too easy to slip into making value judgements or using other terms or expressions of opinion that aren't supported by the evidence you have.

Value judgements are statements that reflect the views and values of an individual rather than any objective reality.

Someone who supports a cause calls it a pressure group; but to a person who disagrees with it, its followers are 'activists'. 'Conservationists' may be called 'tree-huggers', 'freedom fighters' may be 'terrorists' and vice versa. The words don't just have a meaning, they imply an attitude and quite often, it's negative. In a discussion, how valuable or 'true' is the claim that 'Teenagers are unreliable, unpredictable and unable to accept responsibility for their actions'? Value judgements are subjective, often biased opinions. It's important for your conclusions to be objective and supported by facts.

brilliant definitions

Fallacy

A fault in logic or thinking that means that an argument is incorrect.

Bias

Information that emphasises just one viewpoint or position.

Propaganda

False or incomplete information that supports a (usually) extreme political or moral view.

Fallacies and biased presentations

Critical thinking demands a sensitivity to language. Arguments and discussions are mostly reasoned, dispassionate affairs, but even in such contexts, the choice of words reveals more than the speaker or writer sometimes suspects. If you can spot them, you'll be able to think not just about the argument itself but also about the way it's being conducted. If troops are massing on a border, it's perhaps legitimate to talk of them being a 'threat'. But if you add the word 'sinister', you're making assumptions about the reasons why they're moving into position and speculating on their intentions. In other words, you're not just an observer but someone who's becoming involved in the processes taking place.

The obvious areas in which faulty logic and debating tricks are used are those of advertising and politics. Analysing the methods of persuasion and misdirection they use is a useful way of practising your critical skills.

As well as being aware of how others use words, try to balance your own style and choose your words with care. It's very easy to slip into bad habits. 'Absolutes' such as 'always', 'never', 'all', 'every' are such familiar expressions that we can use them without really thinking of how they affect our meaning. Each of them means that there are no exceptions. You should only use them if you're absolutely sure of facts that imply 100 per cent certainty.

A review of critical thinking

- It should be obvious by now that critical thinking is a practical, hands-on process, not just abstract theorising. So make sure you appreciate and apply those practical aspects. Focus on the task in hand. Once you start reading around a subject or discussing it with others, it's easy to get distracted and stray from the point.

- Write down your thoughts. As you do so, you'll be forced to clarify them and maybe refine them. Apart from that, even though we think we'll remember a good idea, it often drifts away and we can't recall it. So make it permanent; write it down. As you review it later, you'll see it more critically and it can lead you to fresh ideas.

- Lots of students lose marks because they simply quote facts or statements, without trying to explain their importance and context or even say why they've included them.

That suggests that they maybe don't understand what a quotation means or implies. Your work will be more interesting and persuasive if it's analytical, not descriptive.

- When you do quote evidence from other sources, it's very important to use appropriate citations. This shows you've read relevant source material and helps you to avoid plagiarism. Make sure you find out which style conventions your university uses and be consistent in how you use them.

- Refresh and expand your own ideas by discussing things with others – staff and students. They might have interpretations and opinions which haven't occurred to you. Bounce ideas off one another.

- Keep an open mind. You may start with preconceived ideas or sound convictions about a topic, but try to be receptive to the ideas of others. You may find that your conviction isn't as secure as you first thought.

- And if there's not enough evidence to support any conclusion, say so. There may well be times when both sides of an argument are equally persuasive. Recognising that is as valid as deciding that one side or the other is 'correct'.

Critical thinking isn't just an academic exercise, it's about who you are. Shallow thinkers rush to conclusions, generalise, over-simplify. They make the arguments personal, resort to stereotypes, make value judgements and hide behind fallacies. Their results are usually inconclusive and unsatisfactory.

To think more deeply you need to keep asking yourself questions, even if the topic's been sorted out or you feel you understand it. Look beneath the surface. Decide whether the sources you're using are dealing with facts or opinions; look out for assumptions, including your own; think about why writers write the way they do. And when you quote from a source, don't just repeat what it's saying, focus on what it means.

What next?

Practise seeing both sides ...

... of an argument. Choose a topic, maybe something you feel strongly about. Write down the supporting arguments for both sides, paying particular attention to the arguments opposite to your own.

Look at the instruction words ...

... in past exam papers. Which ones are used most frequently? What exactly are they asking you to do and what level of thinking will you need to show in your exam answers? If you're unsure about any aspect of it all, ask a subject tutor to explain.

Look into the often entertaining world of fallacies ...

... and biased arguments. There are websites that list different types of them with examples. Just type 'fallacy' or 'logical fallacies' in a search engine; you'll learn from what you read, it'll help to improve your analytical and debating skills. And it'll probably make you laugh.

brilliant recap

- Critical thinking is good, creative thinking.
- There are six steps in learning and thinking: knowledge, comprehension, application, analysis, synthesis, evaluation.
- Understand the various steps for critical thinking – identify the problem, decide on an approach, build a case, use supporting evidence, draw your conclusion.
- Avoid pitfalls such as faulty logic and bias.
- Develop critical thinking as a practical skill.

PART 3

Getting ready
to write

CHAPTER 8

The bare bones of academic writing structures

Whichever type of writing assignment you've been set, you'll structure it according to a basic format to which we've already referred. It starts with the general (the introduction), moves on to the specific (the main body) and then back again to the general (the conclusion). We're now going to look at this structure and examine its elements in more detail.

The basic format

That three-part organisation is, of course, an over-simplification and we need to look in more detail of how each element functions. We'll suggest how you might organise your writing within it and then survey some other academic formats in the next chapter.

Introduction

This is the first contact your reader makes with you, so you want to create a good impression. It needs to be clear and organised and tell him what to expect in the pages that follow. It gives him an idea of how you handle language and helps him to focus on what you're going to write and the direction in which you'll be taking him. So, in overall terms, it needs to do three things:

1   Give a brief general explanation of the topic and its context.

2   Outline what you understand it to mean.

3   Describe how you're going to approach it.

Part of the third point may be that you warn the reader that you'll be concentrating on certain aspects of the subject rather than giving an exhaustive account of all of it. This may be because it's a complex issue and, if you're having to work to a word limit, you can't do justice to all its aspects. Whatever the reason, it's important to indicate this to the reader/marker so that he understands exactly what to expect and why. You can acknowledge that there are many strands to the topic but explain that you're going to focus on what you consider to be the important ones in the context of the question.

When you've finished writing the assignment, revisit your introduction to make sure it's still an accurate description of what you've actually done. As you write the main body of the text, new ideas often occur and it's easy to get drawn into exploring them. This is fine but if that does happen you need to alter the introduction to accommodate those new directions.

brilliant tip

You may have a good idea of what your argument will be but, until you've written the whole text, you can't be absolutely sure of the points you'll make or the balance you achieve between them. For this reason, it might help you to leave the introduction until you've written the main body of your assignment. Once you know what you've said, you'll find it much easier to introduce it. So, if you're struggling with the introduction, consider a different writing sequence: main body, conclusion, introduction.

Main body

This section consists of all the points you'll be making in your argument and presentation of the materials. Its structure indicates how you're organising the content. As you move from point to point, you may need to generalise, describe, define or give examples as part of your analysis. Try to be as clear and brief as you can, and always keep the reader with you by giving plenty of indications (using signpost words) of any changes of direction, the introduction of new themes or opposing arguments.

As you're writing your first draft, you may find sub-headings useful. They help to keep you focused on exactly where you are in the development of your argument and stop you wandering off the point or getting out of sequence. In most disciplines, they're not acceptable in the final draft which you hand in, but that's not a problem because you can replace them with a topic sentence, which will act as a link with the previous paragraph or an indication of a change of emphasis or direction.

Conclusion

This summarises everything that's gone before. It ties up any loose ends and reminds the reader of where he's been and what the main conclusions are. Once again, it can consist of three elements:

1   A reminder of the question and the important features on which you've concentrated.

2   A summary of the specific evidence you've presented to support your views.

3   A statement of your overall viewpoint.

Its function is obviously different from that of the introduction and so is its language. In the introduction, you should try to be clear and avoid jargon or technical words as far as possible.

But, since you've probably used technical or more sophisticated terms in the main body as you looked at the subject in more detail, it's appropriate to use that more complex terminology in the conclusion. Don't introduce any new ideas at this stage; your conclusion should be a distillation of the points you've covered in the main body.

Sometimes students rush their conclusion. It might be because there are other things they have to do, or they're fed up with the subject, or they're tired or perhaps just relieved to be near the end of it. Resist this temptation. The conclusion is the thing that creates the final impression in the mind of your reader/marker. Give it your full attention and leave some time after you've written it to look back over it and check that it's correct and has the impact you want.

brilliant tip

As you're writing, you'll get absorbed in each stage of the argument and its presentation. The points you're making will be very clear to you but when you move to the next point, that takes over and, when you get to the end, you won't have such a distinct idea of each step you've taken. So, at the end of each phase of your argument, try jotting down its main ideas and your 'mini-conclusions' about them. If you write them on a separate piece of paper, you'll have a ready-made outline of the main body which will be the perfect plan of your overall conclusion.

Keep the right balance

It would obviously be absurd to have an introduction which covered the same number of pages as the main body, or a conclusion consisting of three lines. The most substantial (and longest) element of your writing should, of course, be the main body. There are no hard and fast rules about the length of the introduction or conclusion but they should be as short as you can reasonably make them without leaving out essential information. It's all too easy to sweat over the introduction and spend time outlining the context and anticipating points then leave yourself too little time and space to deal with the rest of the essay and the conclusion. Keep the proportions right.

Word limits

Tutors set word limits to essays not to save them having to mark acres of text but to train you to be precise and concise in your writing. The limit forces you to analyse the topic more carefully to decide what to keep in and what to leave out.

It's important to note that falling short of the word limit is just as bad as going over it. Some students keep a running total of words they've used and as soon as they reach the minimum word limit, they stop abruptly. This is not a good approach. It unbalances the overall piece and simply gives the impression that you've run out of ideas. The ending's poor and many points may be left unresolved.

Word count shouldn't really feature when you're writing your first draft. Make it part of the reviewing and editing process. That's when you cut and reshape your writing to make it tighter and clearer.

It's always better to write too much and then have to cut than to write too little and try to pad it out. If your text is seriously past the limit, it might be possible to make an appendix. You could choose some elements to cut, then shorten them and reformat them as bullet points. They're still included in the word count but bullet pointing them makes them shorter. You can then add them to the end of the essay as an appendix (or, if there's more than one, several appendices). All it needs is a note in the main body telling the reader that there's further information on a particular point in Appendix A (or whichever the relevant appendix is). Before trying this, though, make sure it's acceptable in your department. Check your course handbook or ask a member of staff.

Another way to reduce the count is by thinking about citations. In many disciplines you're expected to include references to publications or experts in your field of study. In Law, this could be cases; in the Arts and Humanities, it could be work by a distinguished academic. But you don't have to quote long pieces of text. Summarise their ideas in your own words (but make sure you acknowledge your source). It's all part of developing the necessary writing skills and techniques.

brilliant tip

Most word processors count the words for you. Microsoft Word also has a 'floating' toolbar which shows the total as you write or edit. To access it, go to the Tools menu and choose Tools > Word Count > Show Toolbar. But be careful; looking at it after every few sentences wastes time.

What next?

To help you get the right balance ...

... in your writing, look at chapters in textbooks and see how much space they give to introducing the chapter and drawing conclusions.

Look at some of your own old exercises ...

... or even recent ones and try to identify whether you've included the basic elements and sub-elements of the standard writing format we've identified. Is there a clear division between the introduction, main body and conclusion? What's the balance like between them? Does the introduction cover context, specific focus and statement of intent? Does the conclusion state your position clearly with the reasons why you've arrived at it? If any of the answers to these questions is 'no', work out how you could improve things. It's all part of improving your own writing (and thinking) style.

Take a piece of your own writing ...

... or a textbook which has sub-headings and practise converting them into topic sentences. Decide which is more effective – the topic sentence or the original sub-heading and think about why you chose one rather than the other.

brilliant recap

- The basic format of academic writing is introduction, main body and conclusion. Understand the form these three elements should take.
- Always get the right balance between them.
- It is important to stick to the suggested word limit and, if necessary, adjust your text to stay within it.

CHAPTER 9

How to create
a plan

W e've dealt with gathering the material and looked at the basic framework of a typical piece of academic writing. We can now look at how to bring the two together and choose how to organise your notes and ideas into an outline plan that will present them clearly and effectively.

Creating a plan

If there were a one-size-fits-all plan, we'd describe it but, unfortunately, there's not. People think and write differently and any particular approach may suit some but not others. Some plan meticulously, others simply sketch a bare outline. Too much detail can prevent ideas expanding, too little may leave gaps. The ideal is a plan which is devised specifically for the project in hand and has just enough detail to lead you through the argument with confidence and still enough flexibility for you to adapt it as you write.

Establish the main themes

You did your brainstorming then added notes and ideas to it as you read more. The next thing to do is look at the material you have and decide whether there are any themes or issues that stand out. One way of doing this is to highlight all the items that are related, using a different colour for each category or theme. When you've done this initial sorting of the material, think about the instruction word again and see whether you should start organising it on the basis of description, analysis or argument.

The basic structural approaches

You want your piece of work to flow smoothly through its various points and present a logical, structured argument. To achieve this, you can choose one of the most commonly used structural models: chronological, classification, common denominator, phased, analytical, thematic, comparative/contrastive.

Chronological

This is a description of a process or sequence, such as outlining the historical development of the European Union. It's a kind of writing that's most likely going to be entirely descriptive.

Classification

Classification means putting objects or ideas in order. Let's say you're asked to discuss transport by examining ways of travelling by land, sea and air. That already gives you three classifications and each can be sub-divided into commercial, military and personal modes of transport. You could then subdivide even further by considering, for example, how they're powered. To some extent, how you divide and sub-divide is subjective, but the approach does give you the chance to describe each category at each level in a way that allows some contrast. It's particularly useful in scientific disciplines and any context which lends itself to starting with the general and moving on to the more specific. ('Travel' is general, 'a two-masted sailing boat with back-up engines powered by solar panels' is specific.)

Common denominator

This lends itself to topics where there's a common characteristic or theme. If, for example, you were given an assignment which asked you to 'Account for the levels of high infant mortality in developing countries', the implication is that there's something missing in these different countries which results in children dying. So the common denominator is deficiency or lack. Your plan might, therefore, group its material under the headings:

- Lack of primary health care.
- Lack of health education.
- Lack of literacy.

Phased

The phased model is for when you're identifying short-, medium- and long-term aspects of an issue. It's a sequential approach. The example this time is a task that tells you to 'Discuss the impact of water shortage on flora and fauna along river banks'. You could divide the various factors which contribute to the shortages into:

- short-term – the river bed dries out in the summer and so annual plants die
- medium-term – oxygenating plant life is damaged and wildlife numbers fall
- long-term – the water table gets lower and lower and certain amphibious species decline.

Analytical

Analysis means examining a topic in depth and it's used to consider complex issues. Suppose you were asked to 'Evaluate potential solutions to the problem of identity theft'. Your approach might follow an outline plan like this:

- Define identity theft, and give an example.
- Explain why it's difficult to control.
- Outline legal and practical solutions to the problem.
- Weigh up the advantages and disadvantages of each.
- Say which ones you would favour and why.

brilliant tip

Analysis is useful for many kinds of essays, reports, projects and case studies and also when you can't identify themes or trends. There's a method called the SPSER model, which stands for Situation, Problem, Solution, Evaluation, Recommendation. It works as follows:

- Situation: describe the context and give a brief history.
- Problem: describe or define the problem.
- Solution: describe and explain the possible solution(s).
- Evaluation: identify the positive and negative features for each solution and give evidence and/or reasons to support your viewpoint.
- Recommendation: identify the best option in your opinion and say how you came to your conclusion. (This element may be omitted, depending on whether you're asked to provide a recommendation or not.)

Thematic

This is similar to the phased approach, but in this case the identifying characteristics are not sequences but themes. Each question will produce its own themes but possible examples could be:

- social, economic or political factors
- age, income and health considerations
- gas, electricity, oil, water and wind power.

Comparative/contrastive

Comparing and contrasting derives from the themed approach. For example, consider a task that asks you to 'Discuss the arguments for and against the introduction of car-free city centres'. It's the perfect opportunity for using a grid-style way of organising your notes into positive and negative aspects for the main interested parties in the debate.

	Positive aspects (P)	Negative aspects (N)
Pedestrians	Greater safety, clean.	Lengthy walk, poor parking.
Drivers	Less stress; park and ride facilities.	High parking fees; expensive public transport.
Commercial enterprises	Quicker access for deliveries.	Loss of trade to more accessible out-of-town shopping centres.
Local authority	Reduces emissions.	Cost of park and ride.
Police	Easier to police.	Reliance on foot patrols.

Interestingly, you can write your assignment in two different ways using this plan. The introduction and conclusion will be similar in each case, but the way of constructing the main body will be different.

1   After the introduction, move vertically down the 'positive' column. Now do the same with the 'negative' column, then write a short conclusion to establish the balance between them. (So the main body sequence is: P1, P2, P3, P4, P5, N1, N2, N3, N4, N5.)

2   After the introduction, look at pedestrians and examine the positive and then the negative aspects for them. Now do the same with each of the other categories of people, then write your conclusion. (The main body sequence this time is P1, N1, P2, N2, P3, N3, P4, N4, P5, N5.)

brilliant tip

The choice is yours. However, be careful if you're using this approach in an exam. If you use the first method (P1, P2, P3, etc.) you may run out of time and either not get to the negative aspects or will maybe have to rush them, which will make your answer unbalanced. On the other hand, using the second method in the same circumstances might mean that you don't get round to considering the attitudes of the local authority or the police.

Expanding your outline

The outline plan is the basis for what you write. Follow it through, making sure you don't miss out any points. Check, too, that the links between sections that you noted in the plan are clear in the text so that the reader is led logically through your argument.

Try for balance

It may be that you have consciously to discard some of the techniques you used at school. The tendency there is for written work to be descriptive rather than analytical. You can still be descriptive but be careful to restrict it to just what's needed for the task and, if the instruction requires you to analyse or argue, make sure this is the main focus of what you write.

Explain your approach

The models we've described are fairly standard and easily recognisable approaches to academic writing assignments, but it's still important to tell your reader early on, usually in your introduction, which one you intend to use.

Write 'your' answer

In subjects with a mathematical content, there are clearly correct and incorrect answers, but in many other disciplines this isn't the case and so you're not looking for the 'right' answer but 'your' answer. The way you handle the subject, structure your argument and provide evidence to support it is what counts, and that's what determines the sort of mark you'll get.

What next?

Look at a chapter in a basic textbook ...

... and analyse the structural approach the author has taken. Note how much space she gives to 'scene-setting' using description and to the other components of the text, such as analysis, argument and evaluation.

Read over some of the essay titles ...

... or report assignments you've been set and try to decide which of the approaches we've been describing might be best for each one.

Take some of your coursework tasks ...

... or past exam papers and find the ones that have been framed as questions. Now try converting them into 'instruction' tasks and decide which of the do–describe–analyse–argue categories they fit into.

brilliant recap

- Establish and highlight the main themes that will make up your plan.

- Choose one of the seven basic structural approaches to written assignments: chronological, classification, common denominator, phased, analytical, thematic, comparative/contrastive.

- Expand the plan you've chosen into your answer.

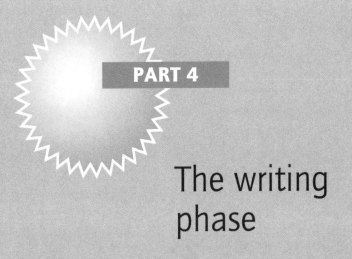

PART 4

The writing
phase

CHAPTER 10

The conventions of academic writing

As we warned in the introduction, the book you're reading is definitely NOT written in an academic style. Its aim is to be more or less conversational, addressing you personally and using contractions (you're, we've, this'll, etc.) to create a fairly relaxed reading experience. Academic writing has its own aims and the appropriate conventions to help to achieve them. Success at university will depend upon you recognising those conventions and learning how to use them. So now we'll attempt to define the basic aspects of academic style and language and suggest what you should and shouldn't do.

Academic language and conventions

Most of the ways you'll be assessed at university will involve the submission of a piece of written work. It could be an essay, a report, a project portfolio, a case study, a dissertation or several other forms of linguistic presentation. Whatever they are, you'll have to write them all in an appropriate academic style. There'll be some differences between 'scientific' and 'humanities' styles but they both share some common features and that's what we'll focus on.

Academic style

As soon as they hear the words 'academic style' many people immediately assume that it means convoluted sentences, long words and boredom. That may be true of the worst types of academic writing, but it's a false assumption. Basically, academic style aims to use language precisely and objectively to express ideas. It must be grammatically correct, and it's more formal than the styles you find in novels, newspapers, emails and everyday conversation. But it still aims to be clear and simple. Most of all, it avoids illogical or emotionally charged expressions and presents its findings objectively. Its tone is impersonal, its vocabulary succinct and 'correct'.

brilliant tip

The academic world thrives on sharing research and learning and there's an old gag that says that the USA and Britain are 'two countries divided by a single language'. Academic writing in the UK is nearly always in British English (BE) but you'll probably read lots of material written in American English (AE). The obvious differences are in spelling – 'colour' (BE) and 'color' (AE) – but there are also differences in vocabulary. In the USA, your 'lecturer' (BE) is your 'professor' (AE) and an author may write 'we have gotten results' (AE) rather than 'we have obtained results' (BE). Some disciplines are trying to standardise their terminology. In chemistry, for example, 'sulphur' (BE) is now spelt 'sulfur' (AE) on both sides of the Atlantic. The differences don't pose a problem but you should be aware of them.

The need to be objective

However enthusiastic you are about a subject, you mustn't let your personal feelings show through. Apart from anything else, they might cloud your reasoning and create an impression of bias when what you're supposed to be doing is presenting a reasoned, balanced analysis or report. The important thing is the substance of your argument; therefore you need to use impersonal language. So don't use personal pronouns (i.e. words such as 'I', 'me', 'you', 'we', us) and use the passive rather than the active voice (in other words, write about the action, not who's doing whatever it is).

To make this clearer, let's look at some examples:

● 'Pressure was applied to the wound to stem the bleeding' is passive.

● 'We applied pressure to the wound to stem the bleeding' is active.

● 'The results were compared with those of the previous experiment' is passive.

● 'I compared the results with those of the previous experiment' is active.

In each case, the second example may seem clearer, more 'natural', but you could also argue that starting with 'we' or 'I' puts the emphasis on who's doing it rather than on the action. By getting rid of 'we' or 'I', the passive construction keeps the emphasis clinical, dispassionate, 'factual'.

We noted earlier that grammar checkers in some word-processing packages tend to pick up passive constructions and imply that they're somehow 'wrong' and should be made active. Ignore that advice.

You can also achieve objectivity by changing the verb in the sentence to a noun, so that:

● 'I **applied** pressure to the wound to stem the bleeding' becomes: 'The **application** of pressure to the wound stemmed the bleeding'

- 'We **compared** the results with those of the previous experiment' becomes: 'A **comparison** was made with the results of the previous experiment'.

(In each case, the noun and verb are in bold.)

There are also other ways of maintaining an impersonal style. For general statements, you can use a structure such as 'it is ...', 'there is ...' or 'there are ...' to introduce sentences. But be careful. Look at this sequence, for instance:

Statistics show that survival rates among casualties are higher when the preferred treatment is amputation.
   It is important for the patient to ...

The 'it' at the beginning of the new paragraph seems to refer to the word 'amputation', which is very misleading. A new paragraph should introduce a new point. To avoid this, you need to change the sentence round and perhaps begin the new paragraph with 'The important point for the patient is to ...'

The same potential for misunderstanding also occurs when you use 'this is ...' or 'these are ...'; 'that is ...' or 'those are ...'. Words like 'it', 'this', 'these', 'that' or 'those' often refer to words, objects or ideas in preceding sentences. When you use them, make sure there's no ambiguity about their meaning.

The more assignments you write, the easier you'll find it to juggle text in this way and the more sensitive you'll become to the flexibility of language.

Using the right tense

You should always use the past tense to describe or comment on things that have already happened. In everyday speech we often use the 'wrong' tense – for effect or to add drama or immediacy to a description of something that's happened. Imagine there'd been an incident the previous evening.

It would be quite normal to hear someone describing it in this way:

He's standing there and I'm wondering what he's going to do. Then suddenly, he gets in his car and drives off.

However dramatic the events you may be describing in an academic exercise, you must avoid allowing these habits to creep in. If you were writing a TV documentary, it would be fine for the voice-over to say 'Napoleon orders his troops to advance on Moscow. The severe winter closes in on them and only a few of them manage to survive and return home'. But if it's an academic essay, it must read as 'Napoleon *ordered* his troops to advance on Moscow. The severe winter *closed* in on them and only a few of them *managed* to survive and return home'.

There are times when the present tense obviously is appropriate. When you're describing your results in a report, for example, you'd write 'Figure 5 shows ...' rather than 'Figure 5 showed ...'.

Using the right words

Good academic writers think carefully about their choice of words. They're looking for precision; they want their meaning to be clear, unambiguous. In colloquial language, we're usually happy to be approximate with our meanings. Take the way we use two-word verbs, for example. What does the verb 'turn down' mean? You can turn down your collar, turn down a side street, turn down the volume, turn down an offer, turn down the radio, turn down the bedcover. And the same applies to almost all such verbs – run over, look up, make up, and so on. They're called phrasal verbs and they have several meanings, some of them surprisingly remote from one another. (For example, you can make up a story and make up someone's face). It's the sort of looseness that's dangerous in academic writing and you should always try to find a word which leaves no space for misinterpretation.

brilliant tip

Quite rightly, there have been questions about how to use gender-specific language. In the past, it was almost always 'he', 'him' and 'his'. We said in the introduction that we intended to avoid the problems this causes by using 'he', 'she', 'him', 'her', 'his' and so on in an arbitrary way. If you don't, and you try to be politically correct all the time, you end up with sentences such as:

A lecturer must give himself or herself time to prepare his or her lectures so that he or she can be confident that his or her meaning is clear to his or her students.

That's awful. But just as bad is the 'S/he will provide specimens for her/his exam' format. One way round it is to make the sentence plural as in:

Lecturers must give themselves time to prepare their lectures so that they can be confident that their meaning is clear to their students.

Whichever technique you use, it's important to be aware of the need to remain correct but without creating constructions which are so clumsy that they actually get in the way of meaning.

From non-academic to academic

Let's see how to change a non-academic text into one that's academically acceptable. At first it reads:

In this country, we've changed the law so that the King or Queen is less powerful since the Great War. But he or she can still advise, encourage or warn the Prime Minister if they want.

The points that need correcting are as follows:

- 'this country' isn't specific
- 'we've' consists of a personal pronoun and a verb which has been contracted

- 'but' is a connecting word and shouldn't be used to start a sentence, so the grammar's weak
- the word 'law' is imprecise because it has several meanings
- 'King or Queen' duplicates nouns
- 'he or she' and 'they' are pronouns which don't relate properly to one another and are misleading
- 'can still' is an example of informal style.

If we correct these flaws, we get a much tighter, more focused text:

In the United Kingdom, legislation has been a factor in the decline of the role of the monarchy in the period since the Great War. Nevertheless, the monarchy has survived and, thus, the monarch continues to exercise the right to advise, encourage and warn the Prime Minister.

The changes are:

- 'the United Kingdom' is more specific
- 'legislation has' is impersonal
- 'nevertheless' is a powerful signpost word
- 'legislation' is tighter than 'law'
- 'monarchy' is a singular abstract term
- 'monarch' replaces the duplication of 'King or Queen'
- 'continues to exercise' illustrates the more formal style.

The fundamentals of academic writing

We're going to look at some elements of academic (and non-academic) writing that can cause difficulties or alternatively help you to overcome them. In a way, they constitute a series of *Brilliant dos and don'ts* but it might be confusing to mix them together so, instead, we're organising them as an alphabetical list.

Abbreviations and acronyms

Some abbreviations can be used in academic writing, for example, those that express units °C, m², or km/h (etc.), but avoid abbreviations such as e.g., i.e., *viz.* in formal work. They're fine, however, for note-taking.

Acronyms are a different form of abbreviation. They take the initial letters of an organisation, a procedure or an apparatus and use them as words in their own right. So instead of writing out the World Health Organization in full every time, you write WHO. The academic convention is that the first time that you use the name of one of these organisations or procedures in your text, you write it in full with the abbreviation in brackets immediately after it. After that, in the same document, it's sufficient to use the abbreviated form. For example:

The European Free Trade Association (EFTA) has close links with the European Community (EC). Both EFTA and the EC require new members to have membership of the Council of Europe as a prerequisite for admission to their organisations.

Sometimes, for example in formal reports, as well as using them in this way, you may need to include a list of abbreviations.

'Absolute' terms

Be careful when using absolute terms such as 'always', 'never', 'most', 'all', 'least' and 'none'. You can use them but only when you really are absolutely certain of what you're claiming.

Clichés

Languages are constantly developing and expressions come and go. Clichés are examples of language which may be useful but which sometimes have become so familiar that they're used without really thinking what they mean. So be aware of when you use them and, where possible, replace them with something less general or less long-winded. For example:

- *first and foremost* (first)
- *last but not least* (finally)
- *at this point in time* (now).
- This procedure is *the gold standard* of hip replacement methods. (This procedure is the best hip replacement method.)

In that last example, 'gold standard' is an absurd, counter-productive term. It would perhaps be acceptable in a financial context but has no place in a surgical procedure.

Colloquial language

We've already mentioned this, and we should stress again at this point that the book you're reading is breaking most of the rules we're describing. But, again, (See? We began a sentence with 'But'), that's because we're deliberately using a colloquial style. It has no place in an academic paper. Nor has a sentence such as: 'Not to beat about the bush, increasing income tax did the Chancellor no good at the end of the day and he was ditched at the next Cabinet reshuffle.' A far more acceptable version would be: 'Increasing income tax did not help the Chancellor and he was replaced at the next Cabinet reshuffle.' Colloquial language is vibrant and expressive but it has no place in sober academic discourse.

'Hedging' language

We keep stressing the need for academic language to be precise. There are times, though, when it's impossible to say definitely that something is or is not the case. That's when you can use verbs that allow you to hedge your bets. In other words, you can state something without subscribing to either side of the argument in question or present several different viewpoints without committing yourself to any particular one of them. That's what we're calling 'hedging' language.

It's very simple; you present the reader with a construction which makes him feel that you're suggesting a hypothetical, or imaginary, case. And you do this by using expressions such as 'it seems that …', 'it looks as if …', 'the evidence suggests that …' and so on. You're not committing yourself, but you're suggesting that something is possible, maybe even probable.

You can actually take it a stage further, too, by using verbs known as modal verbs – can/cannot, could/could not, may/may not, might/might not. If you use them with other verbs they actually increase the sense of uncertainty. For example: 'These results suggest that there has been a decline in herring stocks in the North Sea' can be made even more tentative by saying 'These results could suggest that there has been a decline in herring stocks in the North Sea'.

Jargon and specialist terms

Jargon can be impenetrable. Some of that used in the commercial world seems fine to begin with but rapidly loses its impact through overuse. In academic disciplines, however, jargon doesn't always have the same pejorative associations. Subjects use language in a way that is exclusive to their particular discipline and students quickly adopt the terminology because it describes objects, systems, ideas and events very precisely. However, it's wise to be aware when you're using terms which might be described as jargon and which might not be understood by non-specialists. In such cases, you should explain the terms. Apart from anything else, it helps you to be sure that you understand them yourself and know how to use them in context.

Rhetorical questions

As the word 'rhetorical' suggests, these are powerful linguistic weapons when it comes to delivering speeches. They can be useful in academic writing but they should be used with care and not too frequently. If you're in any doubt, don't use them but instead turn them into a statement. For example: 'How do plants survive in dry weather?' becomes 'It is important to understand how plants survive in dry weather'. (And, of course, since it's not a question any more, there's no question mark.)

Split infinitives

The mission of the Starship Enterprise is 'to boldly go where no one has gone before'. That's perhaps the most famous of all split infinitives. The infinitive of any verb is the 'to ...' bit and consists of two words – to eat, to dance, to go – and splitting them means putting another word (usually an adverb) between them. The 'correct' version would be 'to go boldly'. However, although there are still many who deplore such a 'mistake', it's rapidly becoming accepted. Having said that, academic writing tends always towards the 'correct' so it's better to avoid splitting the infinitive in your work.

Value judgements

We've already mentioned these but it may be easier now for you to understand why they're inappropriate for your university assignments. We've been stressing the need for an objective, impersonal approach. Value judgements express views rather than facts. If you say that 'Louis XIV was a rabid nationalist' without supporting your claim, you're just voicing your opinion. On the other hand, if you say 'Louis XIV was regarded as a rabid nationalist. This is evident in the nature of his foreign policy where he ...' you're distancing yourself from the claim and also providing some evidence to support it.

Honing your academic style

If you were desperate for a loan and writing to your bank manager, you wouldn't be all matey or use slang or txt-msging. If you were writing a love letter, you wouldn't use impersonal, formal language and the passive voice. Of course not, because the bank manager and the object of your affections would be expecting a particular sort of vocabulary and tone. Well, academic writing is aimed at a particular type of reader, too, and he'll also have his expectations. So think about your audience. Your readers will probably be marking your work; they'll want to see knowledge, content and they'll be looking for evidence of critical thinking and the correct use of specialist terms and structures.

Don't say don't. In fact, don't use any contractions. It's all too easy to slip in the occasional 'it's' or 'it isn't'. They belong to spoken English (and a conversational style such as the one we're using in this book) but there's no place for them in academic written English.

What next?

It's very important for your English …

… to be grammatically correct. If you're not sure whether yours is good, get a grammar book or type 'English grammar' into a search engine and choose a page which presents material in the form you need it.

Work with a friend …

… on improving your writing styles. Swap examples of your writing, read hers and get her to read yours critically, then discuss your findings. Talking about them will force you to identify exactly what's right and what's wrong. Feedback's a crucial part of learning and you should get it wherever you can.

As you read books and articles ...

... notice how the authors use the techniques we've been describing. Look for examples of 'hedging' language and see if there are other ways in which authors manage to avoid making absolute judgements. The more you become aware of these stylistic features, the more naturally they'll come to you in your own work.

brilliant recap

- The need for objectivity, good grammar, the right words and the right style are the accepted elements and conventions of academic writing.
- Understand the potentially problematic elements of academic writing, from the use of abbreviations and acronyms to inappropriate use of value judgements.

CHAPTER 11

The basics of sentences and paragraphs

When is a sentence not a sentence? What makes a paragraph? How long should they be? Are there any rules about how to structure them?

These are questions for anyone who writes in any medium but they're perhaps especially pressing for students faced with the apparent strictness of academic language and the need to meet particular standards. It seems that most people know instinctively when they're reading 'good' writing. We're going to suggest some basic principles to help you refine your own style.

The functions of sentences and paragraphs

There are lots of excellent grammar books available that explain the mechanics of academic writing. They deal with the many complexities and nuances of 'correctness' and construction. Here, our aim is simply to demystify the process and propose some basic guidelines on how to create effective sentences and paragraphs. It's sometimes frustrating to be told that some aspect of a piece of writing is 'wrong' and not know why. An awareness of the fundamentals and functions of sentences and paragraphs will help to overcome that frustration.

Whatever you're writing – an essay, a report, a dissertation or any other kind of assignment – the building blocks are sentences and paragraphs. But, unlike most other types of building blocks, they come in different sizes, shapes and colours. As we said before, you shouldn't imagine that, for academic writing, the sort you need are complicated structures, with long, involved sentences full of impressive-sounding 'big' words. The brevity and simplicity of shorter sentences can be just as effective. Remember why you're writing; it's not to impress, but to express.

brilliant tip

A good way of deciding whether a sentence you've written works well and is grammatically correct is to read it aloud. Try to be simultaneously a newsreader and a listener. You may be surprised at how much easier it is to hear (non)sense than to see it.

Sentences

These are sentences:

- **Help!**
- Students **work** in the holidays.
- Universities **provide** tuition in a wide range of subjects.

A sentence has to have an active verb in it. In simple terms, verbs are 'doing' words and we've put them in bold here.

These are NOT sentences:

- Bringing the debate to an end.
- Having been at war for 100 years.

Yes, they both begin with capital letters and there's a full stop at the end of each, but the verb part in each (the '-ing' word) is in the form of a participle rather than being active. Try walking up to a group of people and saying 'Bringing the debate to

an end' or 'Having been at war for 100 years'. They'd probably edge away from you looking embarrassed or scared.
The phrases are known as 'dangling phrases'. They just hang
there needing something to refer to because they don't mean
anything as they are. They would if you added a bit more
information. For example: 'Bringing the debate to an end is
the function of the chair person,' or 'Having been at war for
100 years, the states were impoverished.' (Mind you, it's still
not a good idea to walk up to a group of strangers and say
these either.)

Simple sentences

These have at least a subject (the person or thing doing the
action) and a verb, and perhaps a phrase of other information.
Together they make sense as a unit. For example:

- Babies cry.
- Criminal Law differs from Civil Law.
- Plants require sunlight and water.

Compound sentences

These are two simple sentences joined by a word such as 'and' or
'but', which means there'll be two verbs in them. For example:

- Scots Law and English Law are fundamentally different, but
  there are some areas in which they are similar.

Compound sentences should contain only two specific elements. So consider this sentence: 'Scots Law and English Law
are fundamentally different, but there are some areas in which
they are similar, and this is taken into account in framing legislation but the Scottish legal system still defines aspects such as
house purchase and matrimonial issues.' It's obviously clumsy
and far too long. It also consists of four simple sentences. It
would be better to split it as follows: 'Scots Law and English

Law are fundamentally different, but there are some areas in which they are similar. This is taken into account in framing legislation, but the Scottish legal system still defines aspects such as house purchase and matrimonial issues.'

brilliant definitions

Clause
A unit of meaning built around a verb.

Principal or main clause
Like a simple sentence, it would still make sense on its own.

Subordinate clause
Has a similar function to a noun, adjective or adverb but would not make sense on its own.

Complex sentences

A complex sentence consists of a main clause with additional subordinate clauses. In these examples, the main clauses are in bold, the subordinate clauses in italics and the oblique strokes separate them from one another:

- **Gait analysis gives insights** / *into the walking difficulties that are experienced* / *by people who have cerebral palsy.*

- **Social work legislation protects the rights of the elderly** / when they are no longer able to cope independently.

- *Although Britain is regarded as a democracy,* / **it has no written constitution** / *that can be cited as the basis of Constitutional Law.*

These sentences can be quite long and can contain more than one subordinate clause. Too many of them coming one after the other might give your text a heavy or monotonous feel, so try to vary the length of your sentences. That makes the rhythms of your text more interesting and helps to keep your reader's attention. As a general rule, shorter sentences expressing a single idea have a stronger impact than longer complex sentences but if you want to balance two ideas, use compound sentences.

> **brilliant tip**
>
> When two sentences that should either be independent, or joined by 'and' or 'but', or another conjunction, are instead joined with a comma, that's known as a 'comma splice'. Avoid it. 'Fiona is a redhead, Beatrice is a blonde' is incorrect. Instead, you should write 'Fiona is a redhead. Beatrice is a blonde' or 'Fiona is a redhead, but Beatrice is a blonde'.

Paragraphs

There are such things as single sentence paragraphs; they're sometimes used – especially in fiction and above all, when they're short – for dramatic effect. Normally, however, and certainly in academic writing, a paragraph is made up of several sentences. It has a topic that's outlined in the first sentence and developed further within the paragraph. It ends with a sentence that either terminates that topic or acts as a link to the topic of the paragraph that follows it. So a typical structure might be:

● A topic introducer sentence, which introduces the overall topic of the text – usually this would be the opening of the very first paragraph.

● A topic sentence, which introduces a paragraph by identifying what it will be about.

● A developer sentence, which adds more information to expand the topic.

- A modulator sentence, which acts as linking sentence and is often introduced by a signpost word to move to another aspect of the topic within the same paragraph.

- A terminator sentence, which concludes the discussion of that particular topic within the paragraph, but can also be used as a transition sentence to link to the topic of the next paragraph.

---

brilliant example

Hand-shaking is a greeting convention in many cultures. People routinely shake hands at a first meeting. In some cultures, the practice is to shake hands on parting also. This can be symbolic of drawing business to a close. However, in other cultures the greeting and farewell are supplemented by a kissing gesture where the two people touch cheek to cheek. In France, there appears to be some protocol to this behaviour, which is rarely understood by those from other cultures. Salutations vary across the globe and traditions often differ even within one country.

Here's a list of the first words of each sentence with an indication of the sentence's function in the paragraph:

- *Hand-shaking* – topic introducer.
- *People* – topic sentence.
- *In some cultures* – developer sentence.
- *This can be* – developer sentence.
- *However* – signpost word which introduces a modulator sentence.
- *In France* – developer sentence.
- *Salutations* – terminator/transition sentence.

The role of signpost words

The example above shows how sentences are the building blocks of paragraphs. Each adds its own bit of information and some of them are held together by signpost words – words that help the text to flow smoothly as ideas merge or contrast with one another. The list below shows some typical examples of such words and their functions. It's by no means exhaustive but it'll give you an idea of the range available to you.

Addition	additionally; furthermore; in addition; moreover
Cause/reason	as a result of; because (mid-sentence)
Comparison	compared with; in the same way; in comparison with; likewise
Condition	if; on condition that; providing that; unless
Contrast	although; by contrast; conversely; despite; however; nevertheless
Effect/result	as a result; hence; therefore; thus
Exemplification	for example; for instance; particularly; such as; thus
Reformulation	in other words; rather; to paraphrase
Summary	finally; hence; in all; in conclusion; in short; in summary
Time sequence	after; at first; at last; before; eventually; subsequently
Transition	as far as … is concerned; as for; to turn to

Sentences are the building blocks of paragraphs and paragraphs are the building blocks of text. Just as we've seen how sentences move from introducing a topic through developing and modulating it to a conclusion, so your paragraphs build your argument, develop it, formulate contrary views and synthesise everything into a conclusion. So does that mean we can stick labels such as developer, modulator and terminator on them, too?

Well, yes, but we need to be a little more subtle than that. Simply to say a text consists of a topic paragraph, three developers, two modulators, three more developers and a terminator isn't really very helpful. We need to know what sort of developments we're talking about. Are they giving examples, examining opposing viewpoints, describing a process, listing a sequence of events, defining or classifying something, illustrating causes and effects, comparing, contrasting? The possibilities are legion.

brilliant example

There are two basic ways of presenting an argument, which might produce two different types of paragraph: deductive and inductive.

- In the deductive model, you state your main point first, then add supporting information or evidence.
- In the inductive model, you start with the supporting information and your main point comes as the conclusion.

Testing your writing

We've spoken about the length of sentences. There are two ways to check whether yours are structured well. First, simply read them aloud. You'll hear inconsistencies of logic or grammar. Second, if you feel you need to pause for breath in mid-sentence, you probably need to insert a comma or even a full stop followed by a new sentence.

Another benefit of this technique is to show when your sentences are all turning out to be about the same length. This is a common aspect of how some people write and the problem is that it produces a regular, monotonous effect. Your points are all presented in equally sized chunks and it becomes wearing for the reader. Rhythm is an important consideration, even within the formalities of academic style. So vary the length of your sentences. Mixing short and long ones changes your rhythms and is more reader-friendly. There's no hard and fast rule but if a sentence runs into three or four lines of typescript, check to see whether it would read better if you broke it up into two smaller sentences.

How long should a paragraph be? Once again, think about your reader. When you're faced with solid blocks of text with no visible paragraph breaks, the impression you get is that reading might be hard work. On the other hand, if the information's laid out in more accessible chunks, it makes the task seem less onerous. The length of any paragraph depends on its content, of course, but you'll usually find that extra-long ones will have more than one topic in them. So, if your paragraph seems too long, read it aloud, listen for a natural break point and check to see whether that should mark the start of a new one.

And don't forget to use signpost words to help your reader navigate through the logic of your text.

What next?

Learn from the professionals ...

... by choosing an extract from a textbook and analysing a couple of paragraphs, looking for introducers, developers, modulators, signpost words and transition/terminator sentences. Then do the same thing with a sample of your own writing. Is the paragraph structure balanced? Have you overused or underused signpost words? Have you used the same ones frequently? If so, check for alternatives in the list we gave earlier.

Look at your work as a reader ...

... rather than the writer. Ask whether it could be clearer, whether the meaning comes through, whether it's hard or easy to read. Listen to its rhythms and apply some of the tips we've suggested to make the reading experience as easy and pleasant as possible.

Look at Chapter 13 on punctuation ...

... where you'll find tips on how to use commas, colons and semicolons in extended writing. These punctuation marks are important in breaking up ideas in text into paragraphs and sentences. With this information in mind, look critically at your own writing. Try to spot places where it might be helpful to your reader if you modified the punctuation to make your sentences and paragraphs clearer and unambiguous.

brilliant recap

- Identify the basic structures and functions of sentences and paragraphs.

- Understand the differences between simple, compound and complex sentences.

- Combine sentences (topic introducer, topic, developer, modulator and terminator) to create different types of paragraphs.

- Test and improve your writing by reading aloud to listen for inconsistencies in logic or grammar and adjust length of sentences if you're pausing for breath.

CHAPTER 12

Good
grammar

rammar is one of those things that people frequently claim they're 'no good at', and yet they're using it all the time, maybe without even realising it. Without grammar, it really would be difficult to know what's being said or written. It covers sentence structure, parts of speech, tenses, word order and many other aspects of language. In this chapter, we'll try to give a clearer idea of what it is and show its importance, especially in academic writing.

Good grammar is essential

If you want to write clear, logical essays which make sense, your English needs to be free of grammatical errors. Attitudes to how to teach it keep changing but there are two basic approaches: using 'technical' labels such as 'clause' and 'preposition'; and giving examples of correct usage. Both have their advantages so we'll combine them.

brilliant tip

When you get your car fixed, the mechanic may use words such as 'carburettor' and 'exhaust manifold' to explain what he's doing. As long as you know what they mean, you can understand what's happening. Words such as 'noun', 'verb' and 'conjunction' perform the same function for language. They're part of the special terminology of grammar and your tutors may use them when they write comments on your essays, so it's useful to know them. It'll also help when you need to look something up in a good grammar book.

Grammatical terms

We'll look at the sorts of errors that occur quite frequently in academic writing but first, to make sure that you understand what we're talking about (and what tutors write on your essays), let's identify some of the main terms you're likely to come across. We'll keep it as simple as possible, using an alphabetical list, defining the terms and giving examples.

- **Adjectives**: words which 'describe' or give more details about nouns or gerunds: a *red* book; an *innovative* project, a *rude* awakening.

- **Adverbs**: words that add information about how something's done: the student read *quickly*.

- **Articles** (*a, an, the*): have special rules which you should check in a grammar book: *a* shot in the dark; *an* empty house; *the* Highway Code.

- **Clause**: a part of a sentence containing a verb. If the part makes sense on its own, it's called the main clause; if it doesn't, it's called a subordinate clause. Cats eat mice (main clause) which are vermin (subordinate clause).

- **Conditional**: explains something which *may* happen: *If I had the time*, (condition) I would go out (consequence).

- **Conjunction**: a word that joins two clauses in a sentence when the ideas are connected or equally balanced: The book was on loan *and* the student had to reserve it.

- **Demonstratives** (*this, these, that, those*): words that identify specific items: *this* car is fast but *that* one's faster.

- **Direct object**: the noun or pronoun that's affected by the verb: Foxes kill *sheep*. They eat *them* too.

- **Future tense**: explains things that haven't yet happened: *I shall work* until I am 65. They *will come* early. He *is going to* run a marathon. (Note that all of these can be contracted in informal language – *I'll* work, *They'll* come, *He's going to* run.)

- **Gerund**: acts as a noun. It's formed with the part of the verb called the present participle – that's the bit ending in -ing: *Speaking* is easier than *writing* for most people.

- **Indirect object**: the person or thing that benefits from the action of a verb. Tutors give written work to *students* (which could also be written as: Tutors give *students* written work).

- **Infinitive**: the simple form of a verb, consisting of 'to' and the verb: **to work, to write, to be** or not **to be.**

- **Noun**: words that refer to things or people; there are different types. Abstract nouns are things you can't see (an *idea*, a *promise*), but concrete ones are visible (*chair, table*). Proper nouns are the names of things such as people, places organisations, rivers, mountain ranges. They always begin with capitals: *Caesar, Fred, Rome,* the *Post Office,* the *Rhine,* the *Andes.*

- **Passive voice**: used to describe things objectively. It puts the emphasis of the sentence on what's being done rather than who's doing it: *Essays are written* by students.

- **Past participle**: the unchanging part of the verb in the past tense when it's with 'have', 'has', had'. It's usually formed by adding -ed to the simple verb form but there are lots of exceptions to the rule. I have *worked* here for ages. They had *pulled* the plug. He has *eaten* all the pies.

- **Present participle**: used for tenses when the action is or was continuing. It's formed by adding -ing to the simple verb form. The sun is *setting*. He was *watching* a DVD.

- **Phrasal verbs**: two- or three-word verbs made up of a verb plus a particle (which is similar to a preposition). They give a less formal impression than single-word verbs. *Set down* (deposit). *Pick up* (collect). *Write down* (note). *Look out for* (observe).

- **Possessives**: words that show ownership: *my, mine, your, yours, his, her, its, our, ours, their, theirs.*

- **Prepositions**: words such as *at, by, in, for, from, of, on, over, through, under, with*. They link verbs to nouns, pronouns and noun phrases, sometimes with an article, sometimes not: Put money *in* the bank *for* a rainy day or save it *for* summer holidays *in* the sun.

- **Pronoun**: a word used instead of a noun, such as *each, everyone*. The personal pronouns are *I, me, you, he, him, she, her, it, we, us, they, them*. '*I* have given *it* to *him*.' '*All* are welcome.'

- **Relative pronoun**: a word that links adjective clauses to the noun they're referring to. They are: *that, which, who, whose, whom*. This is the house *that* Jack built. Jack, *who* owns it, lives there. Jack, *whose* wife sings, is a baker. Jack, to *whom* we sold the flour, used it to bake a loaf.

- **Subject**: the person or thing that performs the action in a sentence: *Caesar* invaded Britain. *Caterpillars* eat leaves.

- **Tense**: when the verb changes to show past, present and future events: She *studied*. She *studies*. She *will study*.

- **Verb**: the action or 'doing' word in a sentence: They *abandoned* the chase. Quite a lot of students *missed* the lecture.

brilliant tip

You don't need to learn all these terms but you should treat them on a 'need-to-know' basis. Learn the ones that are most relevant to what you need. If you're uncertain about tenses, prepositions, how to use the passive or any aspect of grammar, look up that particular topic in a grammar book.

The difference 'good' grammar makes

OK, we've skimmed through the 'technical' approach; now let's give some examples of how grammatical weaknesses undermine the impact of academic writing. We'll also suggest how they can be corrected to produce a more effective text. Here's the opening section of a loosely written essay whose title is 'Did Napoleon achieve most for France at home or abroad?' The weaknesses are highlighted in bold and the superscript number refers to the explanation of what's wrong.

> **Napolion**[1] **came up trumps**[2] in both French domestic and foreign policies that were **many and varied.**[3] How **you have to think about**[4] the value of these achievements is **the million dollar question,**[5] while his domestic reforms survived after his **collapse,**[6] most of the **affects**[7] of his foreign policy necessarily perished with his imperial power. In addition **to this,**[8] the value of his achievements has to be considered in the light of whether they were achievements for France or achievements in consolidating his own position and popularity. **In this essay I will talk about**[9] his **foreign and domestic policys.**[10]
>
> [11]In foreign policy, Napoleon's primary achievement was the Peace of Lunéville (1801) with Austria and subsequent Treaty of Amiens with Britain in 1802. This achievement was significant **'cos**[12] it gave both France and Napoleon, **not to mention**[13] their antagonists, a **breathing space**[14] in which to collect **there**[15] resources.

[1] The name is misspelled (which is a terrible start to an essay). Other misspellings are at [7], [10] and [15].

[2], [3] and [5] are clichés. [5] is also an example of inappropriate language.

[4] is a personal expression and academic writing should be impersonal.

^{6} is ambiguous – what sort of collapse was it? Physical? Political? Military?

^{8} and ^{13} are expressions which aren't necessary.

^{9} is an example of a personal pronoun being used. Also, you can't 'talk' on paper.

^{11} A transition sentence is needed here to link the topic sentence with the first paragraph.

^{12} is an abbreviation used in speech.

^{14} is too informal.

It doesn't take much effort to remove these weaknesses and produce a text that uses the same material but gives a much more considered and persuasive opening to the essay.

> **Napoleon's achievements** in both French domestic and foreign policies **were significant.** However, **the relative merit of these achievements must be considered** at two levels. First, although his domestic reforms survived his **downfall,** most of the **effects** of his foreign policy necessarily perished with his imperial power. Second, the extent to which his achievements were truly for the greater glory of France or were simply strategies for consolidating his own position and popularity has to be taken into account. **The aim of this essay will be to evaluate these two dimensions within his foreign and domestic policies in the longer term.**

> **Domestic and foreign policy in this period cannot easily be separated. In foreign policy,** Napoleon's primary achievement was the Peace of Lunéville (1801) with Austria and subsequent Treaty of Amiens with Britain in 1802. The significance of this achievement was that it gave both France and Napoleon, **and their antagonists, an interval in** which to collect **their** resources.

Common grammatical errors

In order to make sure you don't make the same sort of mistakes, you need to find out if you're prone to any particular ones and eliminate them. To help you do this, we'll now offer some examples of fairly common errors and how to avoid and/or correct them. If you think any of them apply to you, put them on a personal checklist so you can avoid them in future. If you want to investigate any or all of them further, use the title we've chosen for each as your search term in grammar books.

Comparatives and superlatives

When you're comparing things, there are several traps to avoid.

- 'Most biggest' and 'more bigger' are wrong, of course. 'Biggest' and 'bigger' are correct.
- If you're comparing two things, use the '-er', not the '-est' form: 'City and United are both great clubs, but which is the **richer**?' For more than two things, use '-est': 'Beth is the **smartest** student in the class'.
- Comparing quantities by using the words 'less' or 'fewer' sometimes causes difficulties, but it's easy to remember the difference. If you can't count something, use 'less': 'There was less snow last year'; if you can count it, use fewer: 'There were fewer cases of meningitis last year'.

Relative clauses

The problem here is that, if you don't put commas in the right places, the sentence can mean different things. Few people, for example, would argue with the sentence 'Toys which are dangerous should not be given to children'. But if the author of it had written 'Toys, which are dangerous, should not be given to children', that suggests that ALL toys are dangerous.

Demonstrative pronouns

These are used to represent a previous word or idea. Be careful, though, because the reference is to the word in the previous sentence that's nearest to the pronoun. If you write 'They were measuring the impact of diesel use on air quality. *This* increases in the rush-hour', it may give the impression that it's air quality which increases in the rush-hour. To make this clearer, you'd need to write 'They were measuring the impact of diesel use on air quality. *This impact* increases in the rush-hour'.

Possessives (its) and apostrophes (it's)

'It's' and 'its' are often confused. Basically, 'it's' stands for 'it is' or 'it has'. It is never a possessive; the possessive form is 'its', with no apostrophe. '*It's* time we cleaned the house. *It's* been ages since we last did it and *its* carpets are filthy.'

Conjunctions

These are words such as 'and', 'but' and 'because'. They join two clauses and, in academic writing, you should never use them at the start of a sentence. (This book does, however, commit that particular sin but, as we said in the introduction, we're deliberately using an informal, conversational style.) 'The results were invalid *because* the sample was too small.' 'The country was attacked, *but* the UN failed to act *and* the member states did nothing.'

Double negatives

Two negatives make a positive and that can be very confusing. 'They have not had no results from their experiments' means that they have had some results. 'The government had not done nothing to alleviate poverty' means that it had done something. The correct versions of these sentences are: 'They have not had any results from their experiments' and 'The government had done nothing to alleviate poverty.'

Past participles

We defined these earlier but they're frequently used wrongly, especially in colloquial speech. Examples of misuse are: 'I'd went to the shop', 'He's ate all the pies'. The correct forms are 'I'd gone to the shop' and 'He's eaten all the pies'.

Prepositions

These, too, were defined earlier and, in spite of the fact that there are examples throughout this book of sentences which end with prepositions, it's grammatically incorrect to do that. 'These figures are the ones the results will be based on' sounds fine in speech but, technically and certainly in your academic work, you should instead write 'These figures are the ones on which the results will be based'.

Pronouns

These are used to replace nouns: 'The results are ready; *they* will be published tomorrow.' Problems mainly arise with the singular pronouns: anybody, anyone, anything, each, either, everybody, everyone, everything, neither, nobody, no one, nothing, somebody, someone, something. Even though some of them seem to cover plural people and things (everyone, everything), they all take a singular verb: '*Each* of the new measures is to be introduced separately.' '*Everybody is* keen to attend the meeting.'

Demonstratives

Once again it's important to make sure that words which are identifying plural and singular items match the form of the verb: '*This* kind of mistake *is* common but *these* kinds of mistakes *are* not', '*That* result *is* acceptable but *those* results *are* not.'

Subject–verb agreement

Failure to make subjects agree with their verbs is a surprisingly common occurrence. It often happens when several other words come between them. '*The Principal*, together with the Chancellor, *were* present' is a bad mistake. It's the Principal who's the subject of the verb, so it should read '*The Principal*, together with the Chancellor, *was* present'. '*The collection* of books, articles and databases *were* sent to head office for approval' shows how, when plural nouns are closer to the verb, they lead to confusion. The subject is 'the collection' so it should read '*The collection* of books, articles and databases *was* sent to head office for approval'.

Words that are often confused

We can't offer any rules about these. It's a matter of remembering them, and being careful when you proofread your text. There are many that sound the same but are spelled differently (complimentary and complementary, bear and bare), but perhaps the one confusion that crops up most in essays and articles is the 'There/their/they're' group. The correct use of each is: 'They finished *their* work before noon', 'Paris is wonderful; we should go *there*', 'Researchers are skilled but *they're* not highly paid'.

brilliant tip

'You get many help for projects from tutors' makes no sense as a sentence. Nor does 'Other students to be frustrating noted the limitation of feedback from teaching staff.' And yet both sentences were offered as 'corrections' by a word-processing program's grammar checker. The originals were 'You get a lot of help for projects from tutors' and 'The limitation of feedback from teaching staff was noted by other students to be frustrating.' So be very careful if you use this facility. If its proposed revision sounds doubtful, it's probably wrong.

If you've had an error pointed out to you, but don't understand what's wrong, ask the person who made the correction to explain it to you. If you can't, check it against the points we've made in this chapter or, for a fuller explanation, use the indicators we've given to search for it in a good grammar book. *Longman's Advanced Learners' Grammar* (Foley and Hall, 2003) has very useful tests to help you identify difficulties. It explains points clearly and includes practice exercises and answers. Another source is *Fowler's Modern English Usage* (Fowler and Winchester, 2002) and more modern, user-friendly sources include the *BBC English Dictionary* (1992) or the *Longman Dictionary of Contemporary English* (2003).

What next?

Identify and understand ...

... your own mistakes. Look back over your marked work to see where the marker's underlined or commented on something. It could be content, structure, spelling, grammar, punctuation or several other things. If you can isolate the grammatical errors and note how they've been corrected, it'll help you to avoid them in the future and could make a real difference to your marks. It's an idea to write down each error in a notebook along with its correction and, if you can, a quick note of what's wrong and why.

Try to learn more grammar ...

... from other people. For some, understanding the technicalities of language is easy. If you're not sure about something, ask about it. Show them your work, with the error, and see if they can explain what's wrong. Sharing is part of learning.

brilliant recap

- To write clear, logical essays which make sense, your English needs to be free of grammatical errors.

- Identify some of the main grammatical terms and make sure you understand what they mean.

- Look at the grammatical weaknesses earlier in this chapter and see how a weak attempt can be turned into strong academic writing.

- Avoid common grammatical errors.

CHAPTER 13

Punctuation matters

ood punctuation isn't just something that fussy people worry about, it's a vital aspect of writing, especially in an academic context, and it helps you to communicate exactly what you mean. More and more, though, corporate logos, advertising slogans and many other pieces of public information are designed to attract attention with unconventional print forms that ignore the correct use of capitals, apostrophes, commas and other punctuation marks. Getting your punctuation right is crucial to expressing yourself clearly and helping your reader to grasp your meaning fully.

Punctuation and meaning

There's a huge difference between spoken and written language. When we speak, we use gestures, tone of voice, pauses and all sorts of other tricks to convey exactly what we mean. It's easy to signal to someone that you're being sarcastic, playful or serious, or when you want to emphasise a word or a point. When we write things, however, it's not that easy. That's why we need to make the most of the feature that does help readers to interpret our intentions more easily – punctuation. It helps us to separate or link ideas, to stress some and give relatively less importance to others. Quotation marks ('...') also tell the reader we're quoting from someone else and apostrophes convey the idea of ownership, as in 'the student's grant'.

The basic rules

Look back over previous work you've done and you'll probably find that you have a particular punctuation 'style', which uses similar sentence structures over and over again and favours certain punctuation marks. There's nothing inherently wrong with that but, if you try introducing more variety by choosing more forms of punctuation, you'll quickly find your sentences have different structures and are more flexible.

▶ brilliant example

Look at the difference in meaning between these apparently identical sentences. It's a clear illustration of how punctuation marks change the sense.

● 'The inspector,' said the teacher, 'is a fool'.

● The inspector said, 'The teacher is a fool'.

In the first, it's the inspector who's the fool, in the second it's the teacher.

When there's no punctuation at all, it's hard to identify the different elements of a sentence and even harder to know what it means. For example: 'the character of james bond created by ian fleming portrayed a fastliving but urbane spy whose coolness was apparently imperturbable he became a real screen hero'. Without punctuation, all you have is a string of words.

First then, let's list the punctuation marks you might use and give a quick indication of what they're for. We'll give more details of some of them later in the chapter.

Apostrophe (')

This indicates:

● possession: e.g. *Napoleon's armies* (singular owner); *students' essays* (plural owner). But note that there's no apostrophe for the possessive of 'it' – *The dog chased its tail.*

● contraction: e.g. *Don't cry; I'm hungry; it's late.*

Brackets (parenthesis)

- Square [...] are for adding words inside a quotation.
- Round (...) are for separating explanatory information from the rest of the sentence.

Capital letter (ABC, etc.)

Used at the beginning of a sentence and for proper nouns, seasons, rivers, mountain ranges, places, Acts of Parliament, titles, organisations.

Colon (:)

It's used to:

- lead from one clause to another: e.g. from introduction to main point, from statement to example, from cause to effect
- introduce lists or a 'long quote'.

Comma (,)

This separates:

- items in a list of three or more: e.g. *tea, beer, juice and wine*
- part of a sentence: e.g. *He came home, ate a huge meal, and fell asleep*
- 'extra' information inside a sentence: e.g. *Rugby, in the main, is a contact sport.*

It also marks adverbs: e.g. *Certainly, the results have been positive.*

Dash (–)

This is an alternative to brackets and indicates an aside or an extra piece of information: e.g. Murder – regardless of the motive – is a crime.

Ellipsis (...)

Marks words omitted from a quotation: e.g. *taxes ... mean price rises*.

In fiction or transcripts of speech, it also indicates unfinished sentences: e.g. *But there's really no room for us to ...*

Exclamation mark (!)

Signifies shock or horror: e.g. *Help!* (But this is rarely used in academic writing.)

Full stop (.)

It marks:

- the end of a sentence: e.g. *This is the end.*
- an abbreviation where the last letter of the abbreviation is not the last letter of the complete word: e.g. *Prof. etc., i.e., m.p.h.*

Hyphen (-)

This is used in a variety of ways. It:

- joins a single letter to an existing word: e.g. *x-ray*
- separates prefixes: e.g. *post-impressionist*
- prevents certain letters being repeated: e.g. *semi-independent*
- joins a prefix to a proper noun: e.g. *pro-British*
- creates a noun from a phrasal verb: e.g. *show-off*
- joins numbers and fractions: e.g. *twenty-three; three-quarters*
- links two separate adjectives or noun adjectives to form a compound adjective: e.g. *greenish-blue shirt; post-office counter.*

Italics (changing the font style)

Used to highlight quotations, titles of publications in citations, species, works of art, foreign words: e.g. *déjà vu*; *et al.*

Question mark (?)

This ends sentences that ask a direct question: e.g. *Where's the library?*

It's not used for indirect questions: e.g. *She asked where the library was.*

Quotation marks or inverted commas ('...') ("...")

- 'Single quotation marks' enclose exact words spoken or printed in a text.
- "Double quotation marks" are to indicate a quotation within a quotation (in British English).

Semicolon (;)

This is used to separate:

- two or more clauses of equal importance: e.g. *They won the battle; the other side won the war.*
- items in a list: e.g. *The treaty's success depended on three main factors: the willingness of signatories to compromise on disarmament; the financial aid promised by the various governing bodies; and the acceptance of a non-partisan military occupation of the disputed territories.*

Paragraphs

These can't really be classified as punctuation, but they can affect your text's layout and readability in the same sort of way. They can be aligned in two ways: fully justified and indented. Check Chapter 11 for more details on this point.

Sentences

They begin with capital letters and end with a full stop, question mark or exclamation mark. If they end with a quote, the full stop comes after the final quotation mark 'like this'. If more than one sentence is quoted, the full stop comes before the final quotation mark. (Also, if a complete sentence is enclosed in brackets, the full stop comes inside the final bracket, as in this case.)

brilliant tip

Parentheses (brackets) and exclamation marks are sometimes used too much in some academic writing. Parentheses often suggest you feel you need to add more detail, maybe even more than is necessary. If you find you use them too much, try replacing them with commas.

It's hard to think of an academic text in which exclamation marks would be appropriate. They're even too intrusive in fiction, as evident in advice from the great crime writer, Elmore Leonard, who said: 'Keep your exclamation points under control. You are allowed no more than two or three per 100,000 words of prose.' So if you have a tendency to (over)use them, try to curb it; a full stop is just as effective.

'Open' and 'closed' punctuation

'Open' is another way of saying 'very little'. People tend not to bother much with punctuation in emails, texts, instant messages and even letter writing. In the academic world, however, where writing structures are often more complex, the preference is for the more traditional 'closed' style – in other words, using whatever marks are needed to make sure the message is clear and unambiguous.

brilliant examples

Open: Dr Douglas M Kay the world famous projectile designer outlined his
            research to staff of the Ministry of Defence (MOD) and the Foreign
            Office (FO).
Closed: Dr. Douglas M. Kay, the world-famous projectile designer, outlined
            his research at the conference in St. Albans for staff of the Ministry
            of Defence (M.O.D.) and the Foreign Office (F.O.).

Lists

Some disciplines discourage the use of lists in essays and
assignments but if you can use them, you have a choice of
bullet-point or numerical styles. If there's a priority, hierarchy
or sequence to the items in the list, it's best to use numbers.
If you introduce the list by the beginning of a sentence (as in
'The reasons for this are:'), you should put a colon (:) after the
introductory words. The follow-on words in the list should then
begin with lower-case letters and each item should be finished
with a semicolon, except the last one, which has a full stop.

brilliant examples

Minimal punctuation: The causes of migration include:

● drought
● famine
● disease.

The list as a sentence: Population decreases because:

● drought dries up pastures;
● people do not have food;
● lack of food lowers resistance to disease; and
● people either die or migrate.

Some common errors

Loose or non-existent punctuation may be OK when you're texting friends, but not when you're writing an essay or some other academic assignment, so it's worth explaining how to use some punctuation marks that students frequently get wrong.

Apostrophes

Basically, apostrophes do two things:

- They show that something's missing, e.g. *It's* not a good time to sell the house. *It's* been up for sale for ages. *We'll* need to lower the price. In that example, three different expressions have been contracted and the apostrophe indicates the missing letters – *It is* ... *It has* ... *We will* ... or *We shall* ... (But remember, never use contractions in academic writing.)

- They indicate ownership, e.g. *Anne's* dress, the *cat's* whiskers, the *government's* proposals.

We need to develop this a little more, though. The examples we've given are for normal, regular words, but there are exceptions.

- As we've seen, for singular nouns, it's easy: you add 's to the end. If they're plural, you just put the apostrophe after the word. 'The *student's* question' means it was asked by one student, 'The *students'* question' means that several students asked it.

- When plurals don't end in s, you need to put 's at the end of the word – *men's* habits, *children's* toys, *women's* concerns.

- If more than one person owns something, the second noun takes the apostrophe – Laurel and *Hardy's* comedy is timeless.

- If there are several people who own different things, you need an apostrophe on each one – *Professors'*, *lecturers'* and *students'* priorities are rarely the same.

In all of these examples, if you leave out the apostrophe, it's wrong.

Finally, two examples illustrating the most common apostrophe errors:

- How much are the *apple's*? (Never use an apostrophe to create a plural – it should just be *apples*.)
- *It's* time to give the cat *it's* food. The second *it's* is wrong. It's stands for it is or it has – as in *It's* (i.e. It has) been broken for a long time but *it's* (it is) OK now. When its is a possessive, there's no apostrophe. *It's* time to give the cat *its* food.

Capital letters

In English, initial capitals are used to name or introduce the following:

- The first letter of the first word of a sentence.
- Proper nouns for roles, names of people, organisations, rivers, mountains, lochs, lakes and place names, e.g. **The Prime Minister** attended the meeting of the **North Atlantic Treaty Organisation** in a hotel overlooking **Lake Geneva.**
- Days, months, festivals (but not the seasons).
- Titles of books, plays, films, poems, music, TV programmes.

Colon

This is used in three main ways:

- To introduce a list, either as part of the sentence or in bullet-points like this. (Note, however, that we're not following correct academic procedure because we should end each bullet-point with a semicolon – it's part of our deliberately informal style.)

- To explain the previous part of the sentence, e.g. The medic recommended a fitness regime: regular exercise, healthy eating, less alcohol and no smoking.

- To give an example, e.g. The quickest response to a catastrophe often comes from charities: Oxfam, Médecins sans Frontières, Live Aid.

Comma

This is the most frequently used punctuation point and yet mistakes are still made. Its main functions are:

- To separate things in a list, e.g. The member-states that do not support this view are Britain, France, Germany, Portugal and Greece.

- To separate adjectives describing the same noun, e.g. I want that big, expensive, high-spec computer.

- After connecting or signposting words or expressions, e.g. consequently, as a result, however, thus.

- Before joining words such as 'and', 'but', 'or', e.g. She had researched the topic thoroughly, but her analysis was flawed.

- To give more information about the phrase that went before it, e.g. The leader of the group, Dr Joan Jones, was not available for comment. (This could also be written as: Dr Joan Jones, the leader of the group, was not available for comment.)

- In the final example, see how adding commas actually changes the meaning of the sentence. 'The spectators who were not wearing lifejackets were swept downstream' means that only the spectators without lifejackets were swept away and implies that there were others there who were wearing lifejackets and survived. But 'The spectators, who were wearing lifejackets, were swept downstream' means that all the spectators were wearing lifejackets and they were all swept away.

Ellipsis

An ellipsis (...) is used to show that one or more words has been left out of a quotation, e.g. 'The educational value of streaming pupils ... has yet to be demonstrated.'

The important thing to note is that you must always use just three dots.

brilliant Do's and Don'ts

Do

✔ Get into the habit of using proofreading symbols (which we discuss in Chapter 16) to help with your editing. Print out a hard copy of your draft text and then work through it, inserting the appropriate symbols in both the text and the margin.

✔ Use lists, bullet-points and sub-headings, but only if your department allows it. The advantage of this is that you can avoid some of the pitfalls of having to punctuate extra-long sentences. Sub-headings can help you to focus on the content and, when you've finished the draft, you can replace each sub-heading with a topic sentence.

Don't

✘ Forget the importance of good punctuation. Read your work aloud the way a TV newsreader would, making sure you 'obey' the punctuation marks. At the same time, be a listener.? You'll be surprised at how many pauses you've failed to mark or you've inserted where they're not needed. And there'll be other inconsistencies which silent editing, however careful you are with it, has missed.

What next?

Look at a textbook ...

... in your own subject area and find and learn from examples of how it uses some of the less frequently seen punctuation marks, such as colons, semicolons, italics, square brackets, round brackets and apostrophes.

If you feel you need extra help ...

... get a specialist guide to punctuation. You'll find plenty in libraries and bookshops, such as the *Penguin Guide to Punctuation* (Trask, 2004). Look through a few of them to find one that's particularly user-friendly.

brilliant recap

- Good punctuation is a vital aspect of academic writing. Its use affects meaning.
- Learn the basic rules of punctuation marks and when to use them.
- Avoid the common errors that occur in essays: use apostrophes, capital letters, colons and commas correctly.

CHAPTER 14

Spelling it right

Spellcheckers make life easy, but their results, although 'correct', may not be right for the context. They can't distinguish, for example, between there, their and they're; pear, pare and pair; see and sea and all the other homophones (i.e. words which sound the same but are spelled differently). So don't depend entirely on them to produce corrections. A far better strategy is to make sure your own spelling skills are good. Here we're going to look at some of the basic rules of spelling and give some examples. We'll also identify 'irregular' words that are often used in academic contexts and others that are commonly misspelt.

Rules and exceptions

English has developed over many centuries, borrowing words and expressions from other languages and evolving its own forms, so it's difficult to draw up a simple set of rules to cover all of them. Even when there is a rule, there are usually plenty of exceptions to it. The bad news is that you just have to learn them. But writing essays, reading books, articles and notes will expose you to words all the time. If your spelling's weak, being sensitive to language as you go along will help you to improve.

brilliant definitions

Prefix

A group of letters placed at the front of a word to form a new word, e.g. 'un' in unkind, 'dis' in disbelieve, 'pre' in prefix.

Suffix

A group of letters placed at the end of a word to form a new word, e.g. 'ness' in kindness, 'ment' in entertainment, 'ty' in subtlety.

Let's start with 20 basic rules and the various exceptions to some of them. By the way, these rules apply to British English but not all of them are valid for American English.

1 I comes before e (except after c). Examples: belief, relief, chief. Exceptions: receive, perceive, deceive, ceiling.

2 If verbs end with -eed and -ede, the -eed ending goes with suc-, ex-, and pro- (succeed, exceed, proceed). Use the -ede ending for all the others (precede, concede, accede).

3 Verbs end with -ise, nouns end with -ice. Example: practise is a verb, but practice is a noun. Exception: exercise is both verb and noun.

4 There are three occasions when you have to double the final consonant:

   – When a word is a single syllable and ends with b, d, g, m, n, p, r, or t, and you add -ing, -er, or -est to it. Examples: robbing, bagging, summing, running, hopper, furred, fittest.

   – With words of more than one syllable when the stressed syllable is at the end of the word. Examples: occurred, beginning, forgettable.

   – When the word ends in an l with a short vowel before it. Examples: travelled, levelled.

5   Nouns ending in -our drop the u in the adjective form.
    Examples: glamour/glamorous, humour/humorous

6   There are several ways of forming plurals:

    – The easiest is when you add -s. Examples: boys, cats, dogs.

    – For words ending in -ss, -x, -ch and -sh, add -es.
      Examples: crosses, fixes, churches, dishes.

    – Nouns ending in -y drop -y and add -ies. Examples: ally/
      allies, copy/copies. Exceptions: monkeys, donkeys.

    – Nouns ending in -o add -s. Examples: photos, pianos,
      cameos. Exceptions: tomatoes, potatoes, volcanoes, heroes.

    – Unfortunately, for nouns ending in -f and -fe, there's no
      consistent rule. Examples: life/lives, chief/chiefs, roof/
      roofs, but also half/halves, hoof/hooves.

    – Some 'foreign' nouns follow the rules of their own lan-
      guage. Examples: medium/media, criterion/criteria,
      datum/data, bureau/bureaux.

    – Hyphenated words make the main noun plural.
      Examples: brothers-in-law (not brother-in-laws), com-
      manders-in-chief (not commander-in-chiefs).

    – Some nouns are the same in both singular and plural
      forms. Examples: sheep, fish.

7   When you add the prefixes dis- and mis- to a noun or a
    verb, don't double the 's'. Examples: disagree, mismanage.
    The only time a double 's' occurs is if the words already
    begin with one. Examples: dissatisfaction, misspell.

8   Suffixes used to form adjectives and adverbs all follow the
    same rules.

    – Adjectives formed with the suffix -ful and -al have only
      one l. Examples: careful, hopeful, skilful, marginal.

    – In adverbs, adding the suffix -ly doubles the 'l'.
      Examples: carefully, hopefully, skilfully, marginally.

- Adjectives ending in -ic form their adverbs with -ally. Example: basic/basically.

9 When two words are combined to make one (which is then known as a compound word), if the first ends in a 'double l', drop one of them. Examples: Well + fare = welfare; un + till = until. Exceptions: well + being = wellbeing, ill + ness = illness.

10 There are consistent rules covering vowels in suffixes.

- If there's a silent 'e', it's kept when you add the suffix. Examples: care + full = careful, hope + full = hopeful.

- If the suffix begins with a vowel, drop the final -e. Examples: come + ing = coming, hope + ing = hoping.

- Words ending in -ce or -ge keep the 'e' so that the sounds remain soft when the suffix is added. Examples: noticeable, courageous.

11 For words ending in a consonant followed by a 'y', change 'y' to 'i' before any suffix except -ing, -ist, -ish and -ism. Example: dry/driest, but dry/drying.

12 For words ending in -ic or -ac, add 'k' before -ing, -ed or -er. Examples: trafficking, mimicked, picnicker.

13 Where there are 'joins' within a word, don't add or subtract letters at the 'join'. Example: meanness.

14 Remember to include letters which aren't pronounced. Examples: de**b**t, **g**nat, **k**not, pal**m**, **p**sychiatrist, **w**rong.

15 Latin words ending in -ix or -ex in the singular, end in -ices in the plural. Examples: appendix/appendices, index/ indices.

16 Latin words ending in -um in the singular, generally end in -a in the plural. Examples: datum/data, medium/media, stratum/strata.

17 Latin words ending in -us in the singular, generally end in -i in the plural. Examples: radius/radii.

18 Latin words ending in -a in the singular, end in -ae in the plural. Examples: agenda/agendae, formula/formulae.

19 Greek words ending in -ion in the singular, end in -ia in the plural. Examples: criterion/criteria.

20 Greek words ending in -sis in the singular, end in -ses in the plural. Examples: analysis/analyses, hypothesis/hypotheses.

brilliant tip

If spelling's a problem area for you, maybe it's worth buying a spelling dictionary. As well as giving you the correct spelling, some of them also list typical misspellings and put the correct versions alongside them. You'll find details of these and other specialist dictionaries in the next chapter.

Spellcheckers

These are very useful aids but at the start of this chapter we noted that you can't just assume that they'll pick up every mis-spelling. They do pick up most 'typos' but, as we said, they work on individual words and not the context, so if you wrote 'The legislators new they had to act', the spellchecker would think that was correct when 'new' should obviously be 'knew'.

The AutoCorrect tool already corrects some common mis-spellings automatically ('commitee' for example, becomes committee, 'cheif' becomes chief). If there are some words you always spell wrongly, you could use the same tool to create a shorthand version of the word which would then be changed to the correct spelling. For example, you might make the fairly common mistake of writing 'enviroment' instead of 'environ-ment'. If you tell AutoCorrect to change 'eee' to environment, all you have to do is type 'eee' when you need the word and you'll never make the mistake again.

But, whether you use these tools and techniques or not, you must still make sure that checking your spelling is part of your proofreading method. Typos and misspellings have an infuriating way of surviving into a final draft so you need to be vigilant.

Common misspellings

There are many mistakes that occur again and again. The incorrect form 'definately', for example, appears almost as frequently as the correct 'definitely'. There's obviously no rule which covers all these misspellings, so all we can do is offer a list of them. Check it to see which ones you're not sure about. The errors are in bold.

Correct	Incorrect	Correct	Incorrect
argument	argue**ment**	maintenance	maint**ai**nance
beginning	begi**n**ing	necessary	ne**cc**essary
behaviour	behavi**or**	occasion	occa**ss**ion
believe	bel**ei**ve	occurred	occ**u**red
Britain	Brit**i**an	parallel	para**l**el
bulletin	bul**l**etin	parliament	parl**a**ment
campaign	camp**ane**	privilege	privil**edge**
committee	comi**t**ee (or comi**tt**ee)	proceed	proce**de**
commitment	commit**m**ent	receive	rec**ie**ve
could have	could **of**	scissors	s**i**ssors
definitely	defin**a**tely	separate	sep**e**rate
development	develope**m**ent	should have	should **of**
embarrass	embar**as**	temporary	temp**r**ary
environment	enviro**m**ent	tomorrow	tomo**r**ow
February	Feb**u**ary	Wednesday	Wedens**d**ay
government	gove**r**ment	whereas	w**e**reas
immediate	im**e**diate	whether	w**e**ther
jeopardy	je**p**ardy		

Common confusions

Another common error is to confuse words which may sound the same (or almost the same) even though they mean totally different things. Once again, we can't offer any overall rule and can only list them for you to check. We've put the meaning of each in brackets.

accent (speech)	ascent (climb)
aerial (antenna)	arial (font)
affect (change – verb)	effect (change – noun)
aisle (passage)	isle (small island)
aloud (audible)	allowed (permitted)
ascend (climb – verb)	ascent (climb – noun)
bare (uncovered)	bear (animal/to carry)
blew (past form: blow)	blue (colour)
board (strip of timber)	bored (wearied of)
born (birth)	borne (endure)
canvas (strong fabric)	canvass (get opinion)
cereal (grain)	serial (in a row)
choose (present form: select)	chose (past form: select)
complement (enhance)	compliment (praise)
constituency (electoral area)	consistency (texture of liquid)
council (committee)	counsel (advice/adviser)
currant (dried grape)	current (present/flow)
desert (sand)	dessert (pudding)
discreet (tactful)	discrete (stand-alone)
draft (first copy)	draught (wind)
forward (toward front)	foreword (book preface)
heal (to make whole)	heel (part of foot)
hear (to listen)	here (at this place)
holy (sacred)	wholly (completely)
loan (money)	lone (single)
lose (misplace)	loose (slack)
lose (misplace – verb)	loss (item lost – noun)
mail (post)	male (gender)
peace (tranquillity)	piece (portion)
plaice (fish)	place (location)
plain (ordinary)	plane (tree/aircraft)
practice, advice (nouns)	practise, advise (verbs)

▶

principal (main idea/person)	principle (fundamental)
root (part of plant)	route (journey)
scene (part of a play)	seen (past form: saw)
seize (grab)	cease (stop)
sight (sense of seeing)	site (location)
stationary (not moving)	stationery (pens, etc.)
weather (climate)	whether (as alternative)
were (past tense: are)	where (place)

brilliant dos and don'ts

Do

✔ Learn the correct spelling of the key words in your discipline. For example, if you're studying politics, you must spell 'parliament' correctly; or in science, you're expected to know that the plural of 'formula' is 'formulae' and that 'data' is a plural word with a singular 'datum'.

✔ Use a good dictionary to check on the correct form of a word. You'll find the word there in all its forms, including the correct plural. And if it doesn't follow the normal rules, that'll be signalled, too. The actual process of consulting a dictionary will also help to fix the word in your memory.

Don't

✘ Use text-messaging language or other abbreviated forms. It's probably second nature for you to write 'C U l8ter' and you may even use it for your own note-taking, which is fine. But it'll be disastrous if you let it creep into any written exercises which you have to submit. It's ungrammatical, its spellings are inventive but not standard English, and the person assessing your work may not be an expert texter, so he won't understand what you've written.

What next?

Create your own spellcheck ...

... memory sheet. Make a list of important words that you know you often get wrong and make sure the spelling is correct. It'll help you remember them and also give you a quick checklist to refer to as you're writing.

Test yourself ...

... on the examples of frequently misspelled words and words which are confused with one another which we listed earlier. Get someone to read them out to you, write them down and check how many you get right. If there are any you keep getting wrong, add them to your memory sheet.

If you're still finding spelling difficult ...

... look for a spelling dictionary in your university or public library. Look up some words that you frequently misspell to see whether this kind of dictionary would be helpful for you. If you think it would, it might be worth buying one.

brilliant recap

- Learn the basic 20 rules of spelling, and their exceptions.
- Spellchecker and AutoCorrect are useful aids. They may pick up 'typos' but they work on the individual word and not the context.
- Check the common misspellings and confusions that occur again and again to see which ones you're not sure about.

CHAPTER 15

Expanding your vocabulary

n earlier chapters, we made the close link between writing and thinking. To pin down an idea or an argument and communicate it to others, you obviously need words. So, logically, the more words you have at your disposal, the more refined and precise your communication can be. In your studies you'll be coming across new words all the time; they may be part of the jargon that's particular to your subject or simply be powerful, useful words you see and hear in books, articles, lectures and discussions. Make them part of your own vocabulary and also use the strategies we'll be suggesting in this chapter to expand the number of words at your disposal.

The power of words

Estimates about the number of words in an average person's vocabulary vary enormously (leaving aside the question of what exactly constitutes an 'average person' anyway). What is obvious, though, is that as you move through school and college/university, your word power increases. You're meeting new ideas, more complex subjects and you're having to exercise critical thinking, and you can't do that effectively without access to new words. As we said, you'll be gathering lots of them as you go along but making a conscious effort to expand your vocabulary will help you to progress even more quickly.

brilliant definitions

Synonym

A word with the same or nearly the same meaning as another.

Antonym

A word meaning the opposite of another.

Glossary

A list of specialised words and expressions together with their definitions. They're often found at the end of textbooks.

Dictionaries and other sources

There are many different types of dictionary, some of which are discipline-specific. We'll look at the main types you're likely to come across.

Standard dictionaries

You may wonder why we feel the need to describe something as well-known as a standard dictionary. Well, it depends. To take just one group – the Oxford dictionaries published by Oxford University Press – is it the *Mini Dictionary*, the *Little*, the *Concise* or maybe the *Shorter*? When we tell you that the *Shorter* comes in two volumes and is 3742 pages long, but is still only a tenth of the size of the full *Oxford English Dictionary*, you may get an idea of just how flexible the expression 'standard dictionary' is.

There are many others on the market, too. Some give words, pronunciation and meanings, others also give examples of how to use the words. You'll find several in your university library's reference section and it might also give you access to an online dictionary as part of its e-resource provision.

▶ brilliant example

Here's a typical dictionary entry taken from *The Chambers Dictionary*, 2003. Edinburgh: Chambers Harrap Publishers Ltd. We've inserted superscript numbers to help identify the elements and letters which introduce various aspects of the word.

Examine[1], *igz-am'in*[2], v.t.[3] To test; to enquire into; to question; to look closely into; to inspect. – n.[4] **examen,** examination. – *adj.*[5] **examinable.** *ns.*[6] **examinant,** an examiner; one who is being examined; **examinate,** one who is being examined; **examination,** careful search or enquiry; close inspection; trial; the test of capacity and knowledge, familiarly contracted to **exam; examinee,** one under examination; **examiner, examinator,** one who examines. adj.[5] **examining.** [French *examiner* – L. *examinare*[7] – *examen*, the tongue of a balance]

[1] Headword
[2] Pronunciation
[3] Transitive verb
[4] Noun
[5] Adjective
[6] Nouns
[7] Derivation

Digital dictionaries

There are two types of e-dictionary to which you may have access.

● Online dictionaries, which are probably available through your university library. They give pronunciations, meanings, different forms of the word, information about its origin and examples of how to use it. For British English, the *Oxford English Dictionary* (OED) is usually available, while for American English, there's the *Merriam-Webster Dictionary*.

- Electronic dictionaries come in the form of hand-held devices, part of a word-processing package or on CD-ROM. Prices vary but you get what you pay for and it's probably best to choose one that has a word database from a recognised dictionary publisher. Get one which gives you meanings and antonyms or synonyms, which are often in a thesaurus function.

brilliant tip

Expand your vocabulary by:

- using a dictionary to check on the meaning of new words you come across

- using a thesaurus to find synonyms for words you already know

- checking the exact meaning of synonyms because there are often subtle differences between words which seem to mean the same thing

- keeping a glossary of jargon terms and meanings of words unfamiliar to you.

Specialist dictionaries

- **Subject dictionaries**: give meanings of specialist terms within a discipline which you won't normally find in more general dictionaries.

- **Spelling dictionaries**: give correct spellings as well as frequently misspelt versions of words with the correct spelling alongside them.

- **Etymological dictionaries**: give the origins of words and how their meanings have changed over the years.

- **Collocation dictionaries**: give words that are often used together, such as 'perform' and 'operation', 'solve' and 'crime' and 'conduct' and 'experiment'.

- **Rhyming dictionaries**: are obviously useful to poets but are interesting in themselves, too. They list words whose endings sound the same.

- **Pronunciation dictionaries**: give a phonetic version of the headword. They use a special set of symbols to indicate particular sounds. The key to this code is usually at the front of the dictionary.

- **Bilingual dictionaries**: are those which give equivalent words from two languages. They usually have two sections, the first translating from language A to language B, the second from B to A.

- **English learner's dictionaries**: are mainly for people learning English as a second language, but they're very useful for everyone because they usually show how the words are used as well as giving idioms and a pronunciation guide.

brilliant tip

Each discipline has its own jargon, which may be easily understood by insiders but totally baffling to others. Don't forget that your aim in writing is to be clear and comprehensible. Be careful, then, how you use your own professional vocabulary. One way to keep jargon words to a minimum is by using dictionaries and thesauri to find words that are close in meaning to the ones you first chose.

Glossaries

Most subjects have terms and words which have specific meanings relevant to that discipline. You'll find these in glossaries at the beginning or end of textbooks. They're useful for looking up what a word means without having to set the book aside to consult a dictionary. Our suggestion is that, as your studies progress, you should make your own glossary of words which are particularly useful to you. They may be technical terms connected with your subject, or words you keep coming across in your reading. Note the word, check its meaning in a good dictionary and write your own easy-to-understand version of it in your glossary. The mere fact of writing it down will help to lodge it in your memory and it'll give you a quick reference guide which can help you to avoid using loose or slang expressions in your written assignments.

If you fold an A4 sheet into 24 segments like this, you can use it as your personal glossary and carry it around easily for quick reference.

A antonym: word opposite in meaning	B	C	D derivation: origin, tracing, word root	E	F
G glossary: word list	H headword: key word for a dictionary entry	I	J	K	L
M	N	O	P phonetic: by pronunciation prefix: put at the beginning	Q	R
S suffix: put at the end synonym: word similar in meaning	T	U	V	W	XYZ

Word 'families'

The beauty of word-gathering is that, when you meet and acquire a new one, it can come in several forms, so you find you've learned not just one, but a family of words. It's important to know which of the forms to use because you could end up writing nonsense if you use the verb form as a noun or *vice versa*. As an example, here's the word family for 'avoid'.

Verb	to avoid	Countries avoid war at all costs.
Noun	avoidance	The avoidance of war is a primary objective of diplomats.
Gerund	avoiding	Avoiding conscription in time of war is something many people strive to do.
Present participle	avoiding	Students are avoiding the exams by trying to obtain exemptions.
Past participle	avoided	Students have avoided the topics that they found most difficult.
Adjective	avoidable	War is avoidable when diplomacy is successful.
Adverb	(un)avoidably	The judge stated that the plaintiff had been unavoidably delayed.

Using a thesaurus

A thesaurus (plural thesauri) lists synonyms and sometimes antonyms for the word you're looking up. The first to do this thematically was *Roget's Thesaurus*, originally published in 1852. To use this type of thesaurus, you look up your original word in an index at the back. There, you'll find several numbered sub-groups of words with perhaps slightly different but connected meanings. Choose the one that's closest to the meaning you're looking for and look up that numbered group in the main text. Many publishers now produce different, A–Z versions. They're perhaps more user-friendly than the original Roget-style thesaurus.

brilliant example

This entry is taken from *The Penguin A–Z Thesaurus*, 1986 (Penguin Books). As before, the superscript numbers are to help you identify its various aspects.

essay[1] n.[2] composition, dissertation, treatise, article, paper, commentary, piece.[3] Attempt, endeavour, effort, bid, go, shot, trial, test, experiment.[4] v.[5] attempt, endeavour, try, have a go, strive, gain, test, try out.

[1] Headword
[2] Noun
[3] Last word of 1st sense group
[4] Last word of 2nd sense group
[5] Verb

Electronic thesauri

Some word-processing packages include a thesaurus. Just put the cursor on the word you want to look up and click on the Tools > Language > Thesaurus function on the toolbar (or right-click for a menu and choose 'Synonyms'). You won't get the meaning of the word but you'll see options for you to look further if you need to.

Prefixes and suffixes

As you know, these terms describe letters or groups of letters which are added to the beginning (prefix) or end (suffix) of a word to change its meaning. If you're familiar with what the prefix or suffix itself means, that'll help you to understand words which might otherwise have posed a problem.

Prefixes

Prefix	Meaning	Example
a-	on	aboard
a-, ab-, abs-	away from	avert, abuse, abstain
ad-, ac-, ar-	to	adventure, access, arrange
ante-	before	antenatal
anti-	against	antihistamine
bi-	two	biped
circum-	around	circumscribe, circumnavigate
com-, con-	together	communicate, convene
contra-	against	contrast, contradiction
de-	down	depose
dif-, dis-	apart, not	differ, discredit
ex-	out of	exit
fore-	before	foreknowledge
il-	not	illegible
im-, in-	in, into	implode, intrude
im-, in-	not	immature, inescapable
inter-	between	interact
ir-	not	irregular
mis-	wrong	misplace
ob-	against	obscure
post-	after	post-modern
pre-	before	prerequisite
pro-	forth	progress
re-	back	regress
sub-	under	subtract
trans-	across	transmit
un-	not	unpopular
vice-	instead	vice-president

Suffixes

Suffix	Meaning	Example
-able, -ible	capable of	readable, legible
-ain, -an	one connected	chaplain, artisan
-ance, -ence	state of	hesitance, difference
-ant	one who	applicant
-el, -et, -ette	little	parcel, pocket, statuette

-er, -eer, -ier	one who	butcher, auctioneer, collier
-ess	female	actress, princess
-fy	to make	pacify
-icle, -sel	small	article, morsel
-less	without	hopeless
-ling	little	gosling
-ment	state of being	encouragement
-ock	little	hummock
-oon, -on	large	balloon
-ory	place for	repository
-ous	full of	wondrous

brilliant dos and don'ts

Do

✔ Learn the abbreviations used in your dictionary and thesaurus. The section on 'how to use this reference book' lists and describes the symbols and abbreviations that have been used. It'll save you time and help you to get the most out of the book.

✔ Sign up for 'word of the day'. Some online dictionary sites will email you a new word every day if you sign up for it. Some of the words may be unusable as far as you're concerned, but many will add to your working vocabulary and it never does any harm to be exposed to words of all sorts. Check the feature on http://dictionary.reference.com/wordoftheday or www.m-w.com/cgi-bin/mwwod.pl.

✔ Use a dictionary and thesaurus when you're writing. That's the best time to pick up new words and check on their meanings. Any time you feel unsure about a word or how to use it, make it a habit to look it up in one or both of these reference works.

Don't

✘ Buy a dictionary or thesaurus until you've checked which ones are available in your library. Look at a few of them to see what information they give under the headwords. It's a good way of checking what's best for you before you actually buy your own.

What next?

Try taking the challenges ...

... posed by some lists which researchers have produced of the words most commonly used in academic texts. Check the lists, find the meaning of any word that's not familiar to you and note it in your personal glossary. The lists are:

● The 'University Word List' (http://jbauman.com/ UWL.html). It has more than 800 words divided into 11 categories. Those in the first category are the most frequently used, those in the eleventh the least.

● The 'Academic Word List' (www.auburn.edu/~nunnath/ engl6240/wlistuni.html) which has more than 500 words and also focuses on academic vocabulary.

brilliant recap

● Good vocabulary is important. Increase your word power by using the different types of dictionary and thesaurus.

● Create a personal glossary as you go along.

● Note the most common prefixes and suffixes.

● Investigate the special online resources which focus on vocabulary issues.

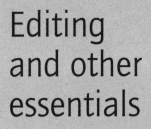

PART 5

Editing
and other
essentials

CHAPTER 16

The importance of the post-writing phases

I f you want your work to be of the highest quality you can manage (and most people obviously do), it's not just a question of being careful as you're writing it, you've also got to look at it critically and objectively to pick up and correct any flaws which may have crept in. Even with the most meticulous professional writers, grammatical slips, misspellings and typographical errors often go unnoticed. The skills we'll consider here will help you to find and eliminate them.

Make your writing make sense

Each time you finish an essay, it's natural to feel a huge sense of relief, hand it in and relax. But the writing of the text is only a part of the overall creative process. The next phase, which consists of reviewing, editing and proofreading, is just as critical and can make a real difference to the finished piece of work. When you draw up your time management schedule at the beginning, try to organise it so that you leave a gap between finishing the writing and starting the editing. That will let you get some distance between you and the work and you'll be able to read it with fresh eyes when you get back to it.

When you do, you'll be looking for lots of things, such as flaws in layout, grammar, punctuation and spelling. You'll be checking to see that it's consistent in its use of terminology and in presentational features such as font and point size, layout of paragraphs, and labelling of tables and diagrams. But you'll also be looking critically at its content to make sure it's relevant and that it makes sense.

It can be a complex process but if you don't do it thoroughly there's little doubt that you'll get fewer marks than you would have if you'd taken some time to make sure you'd got things right. Style, content, structure and presentation all contribute to the clarity and impact of what you're handing in. On top of that, the very act of learning how to edit your work properly will sharpen your powers of critical analysis.

brilliant definitions

Reviewing

Examining a task or project to make sure it meets the set requirements and objectives and makes overall sense.

Editing

Revising and correcting a piece of work to arrive at a final version. Usually, this involves focusing on smaller details of punctuation, spelling, grammar and layout.

Proofreading

Checking a printed copy for errors of any sort.

Choosing a strategy

How you approach this will depend on your preferences. Some people go through their text just once, trying to pick up every flaw in all the different areas; others make several passes, looking each time at a different aspect – grammar, spelling, style, and so on. It's up to you to decide what works best for you. At the outset, it might help if you try focusing on each of three broad aspects in separate sweeps through the text:

- Content and relevance; clarity, style and coherence.
- Grammatical correctness, spelling and punctuation.
- Presentation.

Content and relevance; clarity, style and coherence

- Read the question again and confirm that you've interpreted it correctly.
- Check what aims you set out in your introduction and make sure they've been met in your treatment of the subject.
- Be objective as you read, checking that your argument makes sense, your facts are correct and there aren't any inconsistencies.
- If you've used titles and subtitles, make them stand out by using either bold or underlining (but not both).
- Cutting a text by 10–25 per cent can significantly improve its quality, so get rid of anything that's not relevant, any informal language or expressions and any gendered or discriminatory language.
- Double-check that you've acknowledged all your sources. Don't risk plagiarism.

brilliant tip

You may be surprised to hear that errors and typos which are missed on the computer screen are often obvious when they're printed out. Always use a printout for your final check. If you still find errors, it's easy enough simply to reprint individual pages.

Grammatical correctness, spelling and punctuation

Correction mark	Meaning	Example
⌐ (np)	(new) paragraph	*Text* *margin*
≢	change CAPITALS to small letters (lower case)	The correction marks that tutors
~~	change into **bold** type	use in students' texts are generally
≡	change into CAPITALS	made to help identify where there
⌒	close up (delete space)	have been errors of spelling or
/ or ⌐ or ⊢	delete	punctuation. They can often
ʌ	insert a word or letter	indicate where there is lack of
Y	insert space	paragraphing or grammatical
.... or (STET)	leave unchanged	accuracy. If you find that work is
Insert punctuation symbol in a circle (P)	punctuation	returned to you with such marks correction, then it is worthwhile spending some time
plag.	plagiarism	analysing the common errors as
⟶	run on (no new paragraph)	well as the comments, because this will help you to improve the
Sp.	spelling	quality of presentation and content
⌐⌐	transpose text	of your work this reviewing can
?	what do you mean?	have a positive effect on your
??	text does not seem to make sense	assessed mark.
⌣	good point/correct	*In the margin, the error symbols are separated by a slash (/).*
✗	error	

Figure 16.1 Common proofreading symbols

- Think about how well the text flows and the different parts link together. If they don't, add some signpost words to guide the reader along.

- Check the length of your sentences and try get a balance by mixing long and short.

- Check your spelling using both a spellchecker and, if you're unsure about something, a standard dictionary.

- If, as you read, you feel that something's clumsy, try rewriting it in different ways, moving the parts of the sentences around, changing active to passive or vice versa or finding synonyms.

- Get rid of any 'absolute' terms which might introduce a note of subjectivity.

brilliant tip

Word processors have made reviewing and editing much easier. To make sure you get the most out of them:

- use the word-count facility
- check page breaks and the general layout with the 'View' facility before you print it out
- don't rely entirely on the spelling and grammar checker
- if staff add comments using 'Tools/Track Changes' in Microsoft Word, you can accept or reject them by right-clicking on whatever has been marked for alteration.

Presentation

- Make sure you haven't crammed the text into too tight a space, and that it's neat and legible.

- Check that your reference list is complete, consistent with whatever style you've chosen or been told to use, and that all citations are matched by an entry in it and vice versa.

- Make sure you've included the question number and title, your name, matriculation number and course number.
- Number and clip or staple the pages together, with a cover page if needed.
- Go through all diagrams, charts and other visual materials to check that they're in sequence and labelled consistently.
- If there's any supporting material in the form of footnotes, endnotes, appendices or a glossary, make sure they too follow the right sequence.

A checklist

It may help you to break the editing down into five main areas that need attention. You can then use them as a checklist and work through them systematically.

Content and relevance

- Have you done what the instruction word asked you to do?
- Have you finished the task and answered all the questions it asked?
- Is the structure you've used right for the exercise?
- Have you dealt with the topic objectively, using relevant examples?
- Are your facts accurate and have you cited all your sources correctly?

Clarity, style and coherence

- Have you said what you meant to say?
- Does the text flow, using the right signpost words?
- Have you removed any informal language?
- Is the style academic and right for the task?

- Are content and style consistent throughout?
- Have you used the right tenses and are they consistent?
- Have you achieved the right balance between sections?

Grammatical correctness

- Are all sentences complete and do they make sense?
- Have you checked for any grammatical errors which you keep on making?
- Have you been consistent in using British or American English?

Spelling and punctuation

- Have you corrected all 'typos'?
- Have you checked the spelling, especially of words that you often misspell?
- Have you also checked the spelling of subject-specific words and foreign words?
- Have you checked punctuation and tried reading aloud?
- Are all proper names capitalised?
- Have you divided any over-long sentences?

Presentation

- Is it close enough to the word-count target?
- Does the work look neat?
- Are the cover-sheet details correct?
- Does your presentation follow departmental requirements?
- Is the bibliography/reference list formatted correctly?
- Have you numbered the pages?
- Are figures and tables in the right format?

Reviewing in exams

In exams, you won't have the time to dwell on things, so it's all the more important to make your reviewing fast and efficient. There'll probably only be time for a skim-read, correcting as you go along. If you've missed something out, put an insert mark in the text and/or margin with a note 'see additional paragraph x', then write the paragraph, clearly marked as 'x', at the end of the answer. Similarly, if you find you've made the same error over and over again, such as always referring to Louis XIV as Louis XVI, just put an asterisk where it first occurs and a note at the end of your answer or in the margin 'Consistent error. Please read as "XIV"'. Both these conventions are acceptable and won't lose you any marks.

Reminders of the basics

When you're planning a writing assignment, make sure you factor in plenty of time for reviewing and proofreading. You've worked hard on gathering the material and structuring it, so don't spoil it by skimping on this important final stage.

Review and edit on paper. That's the way your marker will probably see it and it's the best way to spot errors and inconsistencies. It's also easier to make notes on it and it lets you see the whole work rather than just a screen-sized segment. You can even spread it out on your desk and get an overview of the whole flow of your argument.

Read it aloud. It's a technique used by professionals and it picks up inconsistencies, repetitions, faulty punctuation and lapses in logic in a way that a silent reading doesn't. (Just don't try it in exams.)

Try mapping your work. By that, we mean take the topic headings from your paragraphs and jot them down in sequence on a separate piece of paper. It'll give you a snapshot of your text and let you check the order, see whether it flows and whether it's sticking to your original plan. And it makes it easier to move parts of your work around if you feel it's necessary.

brilliant tip

Make sure that you're interpreting the task in the way it was set. It's very easy to fix on one aspect of a topic and focus on that to the exclusion of other elements. It's like making up a different title and working to that. You'll be marked on how you've responded to the original, not a cherry-picked part of it.

Compare your introduction and conclusion to make sure they complement rather than contradict one another and follow the thread of your argument to see whether it strays off the point anywhere.

Too many words can be just as bad as too few. The main point is that the writing must be clear to your reader. If that means taking longer to explain something, do it. If it means cutting something you've written, cut it, no matter how wonderful you think the sentences you're discarding are. Remember that cutting almost invariably improves a piece of writing.

Create 'white space'. It makes your work look more 'reader-friendly'. You can do this by leaving space between paragraphs and around diagrams, tables and other visual material and also between headings, sub-headings and text. And justify on the left side of the page only; that leaves more space on the right.

Neat presentation, punctuation and spelling all help your reader to access the information, ideas and argument of your writing. It may not earn you marks but it certainly won't lose you any, whereas a messy presentation may make your text – and therefore your argument – harder to decipher.

What next?

Look at an assignment ...

... you've already submitted and go through it using the checklist. Look at just a couple of pages, highlight all flaws, inconsistencies or errors and think about how much these may have cost you in terms of marks. This might help convince you that time spent reviewing and editing is time well spent.

On the same piece of text ...

... practise using the standard proofreading symbols. It'll speed up your proofreading on your next assignment.

Practise condensing ...

... a segment of the text. Look for irrelevant points, wordy phrases, repetitions and over-long examples. Try to reduce it by 10–25 per cent and, when you read it, you'll probably see that you've created a much tighter, easier-to-read, better piece of writing.

brilliant recap

- It's important to review, edit and proofread your final draft.
- Choose a strategy which suits you for checking your work.
- Use the checklist broken down into five main areas to help you: content and relevance; clarity, style and coherence; grammatical correctness; spelling and punctuation; presentation.
- Remember the basics of preparing, presenting and submitting your work.

CHAPTER 17

Never ever plagiarise

Plagiarism and copyright are two related topics that are extremely important academically and legally. They may seem complex at times and they're often misunderstood by students, but you really do need to be fully aware of the issues involved. If you don't find out what the terms mean and how they could affect your university career, you could be risking serious disciplinary action.

Plagiarism is stealing

If you take someone else's ideas and pretend they belong to you, that's theft, plain and simple. The problem is that over recent years technological advances such as digital scanners, photocopiers and file-sharing have all made it much easier to cut, copy and paste things. You may even do so without knowing you're doing it. So it really is in your interests to get to know exactly when and how you need to acknowledge intellectual property. Apart from anything else, wouldn't you rather develop your own ideas than steal other people's? Isn't that why you're at university?

brilliant definition

Plagiarism

Using the work of someone else as if it were your own without acknowledging the source. (Note: 'Work' here includes ideas, writing and inventions – not just words.)

Intentional plagiarism is a very serious offence. Universities impose a range of penalties depending on how severe the case is. It may just be a reduction in marks or it could be exclusion from the university or a refusal to give you a degree. You'll find the sanctions imposed by your own institution in your departmental or school handbook.

With such severe possibilities, it's hard to believe anyone would still deliberately set out to cheat in this way. But part of the problem is that you may be plagiarising without knowing you're doing it. It's the sort of thing that happens when you've read something a while ago and actually forgotten you've read it. Then, as you're thinking about your subject, some ideas come into your head which you assume to be yours, whereas in fact they're memories of your original reading. The best way of avoiding this is to be scrupulous about noting down full details of each source as you consult it.

You can, of course, use other people's ideas and words; in fact, it's good academic practice to do so. But you must always acknowledge the source. If you think an author has said something particularly well, quote her directly and provide a reference to the relevant article or book beside the quote. The academic convention for direct quotes is to use inverted commas (and sometimes italics) to identify it as original material taken directly from a source.

brilliant **tip**

We're not just talking about stealing from books and articles. Copying a friend's or a classmate's work is cheating, too. And both people involved may be punished for it. If you let someone copy your work, you're as guilty as he is. So if you're tempted to be Mr Nice Guy and 'help out' someone else in this way, resist. It's not worth the risk.

Cutting and pasting

It's plagiarism if you cut or copy something from a source such as a website, for example, and paste it into your own work without citing it. There are very sophisticated programs now which can scan a text and identify sections which have been copied from elsewhere. More and more, universities and departments are using them to eliminate such practices.

The varied forms of plagiarism

Danny the plagiarist

Danny uses material direct from the source without any acknowledgement. It's blatant plagiarism.

The source reads: 'Most accidents are alcohol-related: 50 per cent are fatalities but not necessarily of those under alcoholic influence (Annual Police Statistics, 2004; in Milne, 2006).'

Danny's version is: 'The majority of road accidents are alcohol-related and 50 per cent of these cases result in a death, but not always of the person who has consumed the alcohol.'

All he's done is rearrange the order slightly without noting the source. On top of that, by not saying where he got them, the 'facts' might just as well be guesswork. A better version would be:

'A study of police statistics by Milne (2006) reported that approximately half of road accidents result in a death because one of the parties involved has been under the influence of alcohol.'

Stella the word-shifter

Stella thinks that, if she just changes odd words and the word order of the original, she's not plagiarising. She's wrong.

The source states that 'post-operative physiotherapy is vital to the improvement in the quality of life of the elderly patient' (Kay, 2003).

Stella writes: 'Therapy after surgery is critical to the recovery of the older patient and their quality of life' (Kay, 2003).

She's simply used a couple of synonyms and reversed two points, which doesn't really show that she's understood it.

An alternative version might be: 'Kay (2003) attributes the improved quality of life levels of elderly patients who have undergone surgery to physiotherapy treatment.' (Using the verb 'attributes' shows that it's Kay's claim, but that the person reporting it doesn't necessarily agree with it.)

Eileen and the missing marks

When Eileen quotes the exact words from the original text, she makes sure she cites the source. The problem is that she forgets to put in the quotation marks. And that's plagiarism.

The original is: 'It could be assumed that undergraduate students wrote what they could write and not what they actually know.'

Eileen's version reads: 'Sim (2006) asserted that students wrote what they could write and not what they actually know.'

She's cited the source, but hasn't used the punctuation marks to isolate the words she's 'borrowed'. A more correct version would be: 'Sim (2006) asserted that students "wrote what they could write and not what they actually know".'

Ed and the missing citations

Ed and Eileen should get together because he's guilty of the opposite omission. He copies words from the original text, puts them inside quotation marks, then forgets to source the quotes. It's yet another form of plagiarism.

Ed's version of the same source material as Eileen is: 'Essentially, what was noted was that the students "wrote what they could write and not what they actually know".' All it needs is the simple '(Sim 2006)' at the end or, alternatively, to insert it at the beginning, i.e. 'Sim (2006) noted that students "wrote what they could write and not what they actually know".'

Sally's strings of sources

Sally's having trouble understanding her subject and isn't confident about her own writing. She reads lots, picks out the bits she thinks are relevant, and strings them together. She's careful to add the sources and hopes that this proof that she's read widely will show she understands the subject. It's bad academic practice, creates text that's hard to read and doesn't convince the reader that she knows what she's writing about. It could also be considered to be plagiarism. Here's a typical paragraph.

'Brown (2000) noted "insomnia is the ailment of the elderly". Smith (2004) stated "insomnia is a function of stressful living". Jones (2001) said "insomnia is a figment of those who sleep for an average of five hours a night". This means that insomnia is a problem.'

It's just a sort of shopping list of sources and she's made no connections between them. She's also failed to see that Jones's comment is different from the others in that it suggests that those who claim insomnia don't actually suffer from it. How much better it would have been if she'd linked the ideas, e.g. 'Perceptions about the incidence of insomnia are varied. Insomnia is problematic for the elderly (Brown, 2000) and for the stressed (Smith, 2004). However, Jones (2001) contends that people who claim to be insomniacs actually sleep for an average of five hours per night. This suggests that insomnia is often a perception rather than a reality.'

Jeff the downloader

Jeff has done the prescribed reading and produced a piece of text. But there are problems. When compared with the rest of what he's written it seems too good, too fluent. It also contains hypertext links and there's no citation. It's an obvious example of Internet plagiarism. Here's what he wrote:

'The incidence of drug misuse is something that invites action from international agencies including the WHO. There are also European organisations that have recognised the need to counter drug trafficking as well as establishing drug rehabilitation regimens throughout the European theatre.'

He hasn't bothered to rework the material – it's just a straight steal. It also shows that he's content to rely on a source that may not have been monitored or authenticated and failed to consult literature from more academic sources. It would have been so much easier to simply write: 'International and European organisations have engaged in tackling drug trafficking, misuse, and rehabilitation. (www.drugfree.org accessed 1.1.07)'

Marie and Tim the sharers

Marie has worked closely with her student buddy, Tim. They've shared material and they've both used the same diagram in their work without saying how it originated. Marie wrote 'Figure 3 shows that ... (diagram inserted)' while Tim wrote 'Figure 3 illustrates that ... (diagram inserted)'.

The diagram was the product of their collaboration but, paradoxically, they're both guilty of plagiarism. It's good to work with a buddy to discuss and sketch a diagram but, for the final version, they should have worked independently. They should then acknowledge the contribution of their partner either in the text, the figure legend, the acknowledgements, or the reference list.

Good paraphrasing

If all you do is change an odd word or reconfigure the order of the words in the original, that's very close to plagiarism. Good paraphrasing shows that you understand the concepts and ideas of the original text – in fact it proves that you're capable of critical thinking. It also gives your reader a broad idea of the key points or arguments without having to read all the source material. What you're doing is free-writing the original, retaining its meaning and possibly adding extra points.

The importance of copyright

When you see the copyright symbol © it tells you that someone is making it clear that the words you're reading and the ideas they're expressing belong to them. But just because you don't see any such symbol, it doesn't mean that anyone can quote it without acknowledging the source. The material may still be copyright. We're dealing here with a highly complex legal situation and what we say can only give general indications of what's involved.

Nonetheless, it's important for you to be aware of the nature of copyright and avoid infringing it. Once again, that is stealing. Under the law, your work is protected and others can't use it without your permission. In the UK, that protection applies during the author's lifetime and for 70 years afterwards. That's why you usually see © accompanied by a date and the owner's name at the start of a book.

So you need to be sure that you're not breaking the law when you're photocopying something, digitally scanning it or printing it out without the owner's permission. This isn't as harsh as it sounds because educational copying, for non-commercial private study or research, is usually allowed by publishers. But it's better to stay safe and make sure you only copy a small amount of material under what's called the 'fair dealing' provision. There's no precise legal definition for this but it means just using very short extracts and acknowledging the source.

brilliant tip

The laws as we're describing them apply to what's classified as 'private study or research' and that means exactly what it says. If you're using the material for commercial or other reasons, such as photocopying a funny article for your friends, that's illegal. So is copying software and music CDs (including 'sharing' MP3 files).

How much can you copy?

It's safer to ask at your library or in your department to find out exactly how much you can copy and what the general copying rules are. In general, you shouldn't copy more than 5 per cent of the work involved, or:

- one chapter of a book
- one article per volume of an academic journal
- 20 per cent (to a maximum of 20 pages) of a short book
- one poem or short story (maximum of 10 pages) from an anthology

- one separate illustration or map up to A4 size
- short excerpts of musical works – not whole works or movements.

In each of these cases we're talking about single copies. You're not allowed to make multiple copies of any of these or hand over a single copy for multiple copying to someone else.

Even if you're copying from something you bought and which you therefore own, such as a book or CD, if you copy it or a significant part of it without permission, you're infringing copyright.

And the same rules apply to text, music and/or images on the internet. Some sites do offer copyright-free images but you should check the home page to see if there's a statement about copyright or a link to one.

brilliant dos and don'ts

Do

✔ Make sure you always quote the source when you're copying material by electronic means. It's only too easy to highlight some text, then copy and paste it into a file and move on. If you then use it in your work without saying where you got it, you could be in trouble.

✔ Write full details of sources when you're making notes. Do this on the same piece of paper that you used to summarise them or copy them out. And when you take down phrases and extracts using the exact words of the original, always put quote marks around them. When you look at them later, you may not remember that they're direct quotes and it's important to acknowledge that they are in any material you submit. You may not use them in your final draft but even if you just paraphrase them, you still have to cite the source.

▶

✔ Double-check all your 'original' ideas. Your individual take on a subject may represent a fresh, unique insight into a topic but, equally, it may be something you read months before which has just resurfaced. Think carefully about possible sources and, if you're not sure, check with people such as your tutor or supervisor to see whether the idea's familiar to them, or look at relevant texts, encyclopaedias or the internet.

Don't

✘ Paraphrase a source too closely; if all you're doing is taking key phrases and rearranging them, or just replacing some words with synonyms, that's still plagiarism.

✘ Use too many quotations. A text which simply strings together chunks of other people's ideas will probably make for dull, uneven reading and will certainly be guilty of plagiarising.

What next?

Double-check ...

... your department's (or university's) plagiarism policy. This should tell you what the rules are and how you might break them. It'll also give you information on how to cite sources.

Read the notices in the library ...

... about photocopying or, if there aren't any, ask about it.

When you're making notes ...

... highlight and put quotations marks around all direct transcriptions. And (yes, we're saying it again) add full details of the source whenever you take notes from a textbook or other paper source.

 **recap**

- There are many forms of plagiarism; you must be fully aware of the issues involved.

- Avoid plagiarising by using good paraphrasing and summarising and using quotations properly.

- Make sure you understand and respect the complexities of copyright.

- Avoid breaking the rules of copyright.

CHAPTER 18

Quotations, citations and references

As we keep emphasising, academic writing at all levels is much more formal than most other types of writing and you need to learn the basic rules and follow them. Many of them relate to how you use and acknowledge material you've found in the work of others. There are several referencing styles and the one you use will depend on your university's preferred option. We'll take an overview of them here and outline the four main ones and how to use them.

Acknowledging the work of others

Every kind of academic paper, from essay to thesis, refers to work done on the topic by others in the past. It's normal – in fact, it's essential – to read widely on topics and benefit from what others have discovered or proposed. And, whether you quote directly from their texts or simply paraphrase their ideas, you must tell your reader exactly where you found the material so that she's able to locate your source for herself.

So you do two things:

- indicate the source in the body of your text at the point where you refer to or quote it;
- give full details of it in a footnote, endnote or separate reference list at the end of your paper.

> ◆ **brilliant** definitions
>
> **Citation**
>
> The use of an idea presented by an author and expressed in your own words to support a point made in your own work.
>
> **Quotation**
>
> The use of words taken directly from the source.
>
> **Bibliography**
>
> A listing at the end of your work of all the source materials you've consulted. You don't need to have used them all directly in your text. In some styles the word 'bibliography' is used instead of 'reference list'.
>
> **Reference list**
>
> All the books, journals, web and online materials you've referred to in your paper. It's usually placed at the end.

Referencing styles

You'll find your department's preferred style in your course handbook, or it may be recommended by your lecturer or supervisor. If there's no stated preference, the choice is yours, so you need to have an idea of the sort of variations there are. That's why we'll now look at the four most popular styles and highlight how they work. To make it all simpler, we'll invent a book, its author, publication date and publishers. Let's be pretentious and call it *The Existential Lay-by* by K. J. Shiels, published by Pekinese Press, Cambridge in 2007. None of the 'quotations' from it are intended to be accurate or even to make much sense; they're only there to provide examples of how citations and quotations work.

When it comes to how you format the source for inclusion in your reference list or bibliography, however, there are so many possible variations (multiple authors, articles in newspapers, journals or in collections edited by someone else, online resources, broadcasts and so on), that it would be confusing to list them all here. Instead, we suggest that, once you know which style your university prefers, you use a search engine to consult one of the many excellent sites which lay out examples of each very clearly. The search term 'Harvard style', 'Vancouver style', etc. is all you need.

Harvard

This is perhaps the simplest, quickest and possibly the easiest to adjust of the four.

- When you refer to the source in your text, you put the author's name and the date in brackets at the end of the sentence, e.g. *Not all philosophies are sensible (Shiels, 2007)*. (Note that this isn't a direct quote from Shiels but a paraphrase of his viewpoint.)

- You can also make the author's name part of your sentence, putting the date in brackets immediately after it, e.g. *Shiels (2007) argues that existentialism and absurdism occupy different points on the spectrum of despair.*

- If you quote directly from the book, you must also add the relevant page number, e.g. *According to Shiels (2007, p. 23) 'dialectical materialism predicated a linear narrative which has today been undermined by the phenomenon of hypertext'.*

- The way to identify the book in your reference list or bibliography is: Shiels, K. J., 2007. *The existential lay-by*. Cambridge: Pekinese Press. (Note that everything, including the punctuation marks, must follow this exact pattern. The same applies with every other referencing style.)

Modern Languages Association (MLA)

- When you refer to the source in your text, you put the author's name and the page number in brackets, e.g. *Not all philosophies are sensible (Shiels, 126).*

- You can also make the author's name part of your sentence, putting the page number in brackets at the end of the sentence or clause, e.g. *Shiels argues that existentialism and absurdism occupy different points on the spectrum of despair (79).*

- If you quote directly from the book, you must put the name and page number at the end of the sentence, e.g. *'dialectical materialism predicated a linear narrative which has today been undermined by the phenomenon of hypertext' (Shiels 23).*

- The way to identify the book in your reference list or bibliography is: Shiels, K. J. *The existential lay-by.* Cambridge: Pekinese Press, 2007.

Vancouver

This is a numerical system with full-size numerals in brackets after the citation or quotation. Each number refers to a work listed in the bibliography or reference list, where the sources themselves are numbered 1, 2, 3, etc. It makes the text easier to read because there are no names or other bits of information interrupting the flow. On the other hand, if the reader wants to know the source of the reference, he has to stop reading and turn to the bibliography to find it. If you cite or quote more than once from a particular source, each time you put the same number in brackets, so if you're quoting from Shiels and two other imaginary writers, Ebeneezer Black and Billabong White, and the quotations/citations come in the order Black, Shiels, Shiels, White, Black, White, Shiels, the sequence of numbers in brackets will be (1), (2), (2), (3), (1), (3), (2).

The way to identify the book in your reference list or bibliography is:

Shiels K. J. The existential lay-by. Cambridge: Pekinese Press; 2007.

Chicago

This style uses footnotes. The first time a particular source is cited or quoted, the full bibliographical information is given in a footnote. Each time it's used after that, abbreviations are used. The sequence might be as follows:

- Shiels claimed that not all philosophies are sensible[1].
  The footnote will read: K. J. Shiels, *The existential lay-by.* (Cambridge: Pekinese Press, 2007), 126. (This means the reference is to page 126.)

- We'll assume that you're quoting or citing from other references and that they take up footnotes 2, 3 and 4, so the next time Shiels is sourced, the footnote will read:
  [5] Shiels, *op. cit.,* 27 (*op. cit.* means 'work already quoted' and 27 is the page number).

- If there are no other references between this and the next Shiels one, the footnote will read: [6] Shiels, *ibid.,* 159. (*Ibid* is short for *ibidem,* meaning 'the same'. It's indicating that it's the same Shiels text you've already quoted but this time the reference is to page 159.)

- The way to identify the book in your reference list or bibliography is: Shiels, K. J. 2007. *The existential lay-by.* Cambridge: Pekinese Press. (Notice that the layout of the full bibliographical information is formatted differently here than it was in the footnote.)

What's it all for?

This may seem fussy but there are good reasons for giving full information about the quotations and citations you use.

Ideas in books and articles belong to the people who express them. They themselves may have got them from others but if you're using their version, you must acknowledge that you're borrowing from them. Even if your aim is to disagree with them, you must still give them credit for what is their intellectual property.

Noting what sources you used will help your reader to understand how you put your own argument together and where it fits into general studies of and opinions about the topic. By knowing the sort of influences you responded to, he'll be better able to place your work and form opinions about it. It will also show him how much reading you've done and the scope of your knowledge of the subject. This will be useful if he's assessing your work or advising you on further reading or sources that are more relevant.

Finally, it'll give him the information he needs if he wants to read the source material for himself.

Reference lists are part of an academic discipline. Quite often, if you fail to provide one, you'll lose marks.

brilliant tip

If you have a quotation contained inside another one, in British English you put the whole quotation in single inverted commas and the contained quotation in double inverted commas. To demonstrate this, here's another quote from our fictional author Shiels: 'Philosophy consists of more than Shakespeare's notion that "There's nothing either good or bad but thinking makes it so" but the words are a valuable starting point'. In American English, that becomes: "Philosophy consists of more than Shakespeare's notion that 'There's nothing either good or bad but thinking makes it so' but the words are a valuable starting point."

Using information within your text

There are two ways of introducing the work of others into your text: by quoting exact words from a source; or by citation, which involves summarising or paraphrasing the idea in your own words. Remember that, in both cases, you must acknowledge the source of the material.

Quotations

In this case, it depends whether the quotation's short or long. If it's short, put the exact words in single inverted commas within your own sentence. If we make xxxx your words and zzz the words of the quotation, this gives us; xxxx xx xxxx 'zzzz zz zzzz zz zzzz' xxx xxxx x xxx. If it's a long quotation, say 30 words or more, you don't use inverted commas. Instead, you separate it from your own text by indenting it and using single-spacing for it, like this:

Xxx xxxx x xxx xxxxxxxxx xxxxxxx xxxxx xxxx:

> Zzzz zz zzzzzz z zzzz zz zzzzzz zz zzzz zzzz zzzzz zz zzz zzzzzzzzzzzzzz zz zzzzz zzzzz zzzzzzz zzzzzzz zzzzz zz zz z zzzzzz z zz zzzzzzzz zzzz zz zzzzzzzz zzzzzzzzzzzz zzz zzzzzzzzzz
>
> (source reference)

Xxx xxxx x xxx xxxxxxxxx xxxxxxx xxxxx xxxx

If you deliberately miss out some words from the original, you show you've done so by filling the 'gap' with three dots. This is called ellipsis. For example, if the quotation in the last example started somewhere other than at the beginning of a sentence, you'd write:

Xxx xxxx x xxx xxxxxxxxx xxxxxxx xxxxx xxxx:

... zzz zz zzzzzz z zzzz zz zzzzzz zz zzzz zzzz zzzzz zz zzz zzzzzzzzzzzzzz zz zzzzz zzzzz zzzzzzz zzzzzzz zzzzz zz zz z zzzzzz z zz zzzzzzzz zzzz zz zzzzzzzz zzzzzzzzzzzz zzz zzzzzzzzzzz

(source reference)

Xxxxx xxx x xxx xxxxxxxxx xxxxxxx xxxxx xxxx

If the words are left out of the body of the quotation, an ellipsis is still used but it's enclosed by square brackets to show that there wasn't an ellipsis in the original, e.g. 'zzz zz zzzzzz z zzzz zz zzzzzz [...] zzzz zzzz zzzzz zz zzz'.

brilliant tip

Cutting words out of a quote which aren't relevant to the point it's supporting helps to keep it brief and focused. But you must never omit words that change the sense of the quotation. If the quotation was 'The prospect of entry into a federal European Union is not universally acceptable', leaving out the word 'not' would change its meaning completely and misrepresent the views of the author.

Citations

There are two basic ways of citing text, one which stresses the information, the other which stresses the author. If we use the Harvard method for identifying the sources, examples of the two methods would be:

- Philosophical advances are almost entirely dependent on linguistic evolution (Shiels, 2007).
- Shiels (2007) claimed that philosophical advances were almost entirely dependent on linguistic evolution.

In the first, the statement reads as if it's a generally accepted 'truth' which he's articulating; in the second, it may still be a 'truth' but by putting the author at the beginning, it makes it seem more like his opinion.

Footnotes and endnotes

We've already seen how footnotes are used in the Chicago referencing style. Their more general use is to provide additional information or add a comment or discussion point which would interrupt the flow of the argument if it was included in the text. They're at the bottom of the page on which the link appears. Endnotes are collected together at the end of the whole text. Before using them, you should check what your department's policy is.

brilliant tip

In the example above, we used the word 'claimed' to introduce a citation from Shiels. There are lots of verbs that can be used in the same context, i.e. to report the views of others.

Some of the ones most frequently seen are:

allege	consider	explain	state
assert	contend	judge	surmise
claim	declare	propose	warn

They don't all mean the same thing, of course, and some are definitely 'stronger' than others. Choose carefully so that it's clear what you think the impact of the quoted or cited work is.

Software referencing packages

These are flexible programs and can create your reference list in several different formats. But, unless you're very familiar with them, does it really make sense to spend time learning how to use such complex tools and keying in the data to 'feed' them? It would probably be quicker and produce the same results if you typed a list straight into a word-processed table and sorted it alphabetically.

Making citing and listing references easier for yourself

It must be obvious by now that citations and quotations are crucial to the production of good quality academic writing. So get into good habits from the start. Whichever way you prefer to make and copy notes – electronically, photocopying, writing – make sure you always include all the necessary bibliographical information. If you don't, it'll take ages to find it later.

Choose or find out which reference style to use as early as possible. Don't switch between systems. Whichever you choose, follow its conventions to the letter, including all punctuation details. Once you've done so, add works to your reference list as you read them. Just set up a table or list and type in the relevant details as soon as you cite the source in the text. Using a table makes the formatting easier and lets you insert new records very easily.

Even if you're not sure whether you'll use a quotation you're noting down, you should still record full reference details with it. You may have an excellent memory but it'll still take time to locate the source and note down its details later. And if your memory's not so good, it'll be a very frustrating process.

What next?

Find out which referencing style ...

... is recommended for your subjects. These may be different from one discipline or tutor to another. Some subjects such as Law, History and English Literature often use specialised methods of citation and referencing. Usually, you'll get some training on what's needed. If you don't, look at the way the referencing has been done in the books on your reading lists. If you compare it with the examples we've given, that should help you to identify the style by name.

Look at textbooks or journal articles ...

... in your subject area to see if they deviate from the four styles we've listed. Sometimes you may find they've modified them in some way. If so, or if you're still unsure about what style to use, ask your tutor about it.

brilliant recap

- Acknowledge your sources by referencing them correctly.
- There are four main academic styles: Harvard, MLA, Vancouver and Chicago. Understand the importance of using such styles.
- Know the difference between quotations and citations and how to use them.
- Make citing and listing references easy for yourself.

PART 6

Maximising your potential

CHAPTER 19

The elements and advantages of good presentation

I t's fair to say that, once you've done the reading, constructed your arguments, written, reviewed and edited your assignment, your work's ready to be assessed. But you don't want to risk creating a bad impression by sloppy presentation. The final checks to make before handing it in are on the seemingly trivial but nonetheless important question of how it looks. It's not rocket science to realise that a dog-eared, dirty, coffee-stained bundle of paper won't be viewed in quite the same way as a clean, tidy, professionally prepared document. So it's time for the final pre-submission survey.

Academic conventions of presentation

Most marks for assignments are awarded for content, but some can be won or lost through how it's presented. The way in which you package and deliver it reveals the degree of respect for and pride in what you've written and if you seem to care little for it, it doesn't encourage the marker to anticipate anything very special. We're not just talking about layout and the use of visual elements, we also mean accuracy, consistency and attention to detail. It's part of the proofreading phase, so allow time for it.

Layout

There are so many different types of written submission – essays, reports, summaries, case studies – that we can't describe a 'standard' layout. An essay could have a relatively simple structure: cover page, main text, list of references. A lab report might have title page, abstract, introduction, sections on materials and methods, results, discussion/conclusion and references. There'll be variations, too, according to your academic discipline and maybe even your department. You'll have to find out what's expected of you before you get started on your first assignment. Check your course handbook or ask a tutor.

Cover page

This is the first thing your marker will see, so get it right. If your department has a preferred cover-page design, follow it exactly. It may have been organised that way for a specific administrative purpose, such as making sure that work's marked anonymously or giving markers a standard format for feedback, so stick to the rules.

If there aren't any such rules, write your name and/or matriculation number, the course title and/or code. It's also useful for you to add the name of the tutor. And, of course, in a prominent position, you should put the number and title of the question. The aim is clarity. Don't be tempted to indulge in fancy fonts or graphics; it won't earn you any extra marks.

Main text

Very few submissions nowadays are handwritten and departments usually expect student assignments to be word-processed. As we said earlier, editing is easier on a printout and a good quality printer gives a more professional result. But if you are writing out your submission by hand, leave yourself plenty of time to copy out your draft neatly and legibly. Write on one side of the paper; it makes it easier to read, and if you make a mistake, you only have to rewrite a single sheet.

brilliant tip

To help you check for 'white space', look critically at your text to make sure you've used paragraphing effectively. If you reduce the 'Zoom' function on the 'View' menu to 25 per cent, you'll see lots of your written pages on the screen and get a good idea of how long your paragraphs are and how much 'white space' you've left. You can use this information to make your text more reader-friendly.

Font

There are two main choices: serif types have extra little strokes at the end of each letter; sans serif types don't. It'll probably be up to you to choose your preferred font but serif types with a font size of 11 or 12 are the easiest to read for most people.

Elaborate font types may look attractive or exciting but they can be distracting and actually get in the way of absorbing the content. The same applies to using too many forms of emphasis. Choose *italics* or **bold** and stick with the one you've chosen throughout. If you need to add symbols, use Microsoft Word's 'Insert > Symbol' command.

Margins

A useful convention is for left-hand margins to be 4 cm and the right-hand margins 2.5 cm. This allows space for the marker's comments and ensures that the text can be read if you use a left-hand binding.

Line spacing

It's easier to read text spaced at least at 1.5–2 lines apart. Some markers like to add comments as they read the text and this leaves them space to do so. If you're inserting long quotations, though, you should indent them and make them single-line spaced.

Paragraphs

We've already noted the value of 'white space'. Lay out your paragraphs clearly and consistently. Depending on your department's preferences, you can indent them, which means the first line starts four spaces in from the left-hand margin, or block them, which is when they all begin on the left-hand margin but you separate them by a double-line space. In Microsoft Word you can control your paragraph style using the 'Format > Paragraph' command.

Sub-headings

These are certainly useful as you write the essay since they help to keep you orientated in your argument. Before you decide whether to keep them in your final draft, check your department's policy; some accept them, others don't. If you do have to get rid of them, don't just delete them, expand them into topic sentences.

Word count

As we're said before, take the word count seriously. Writing too much is as bad as writing too little. If you go way over the limit, the likelihood is that you'll swamp the reader with information and your points may get lost among all the words. Almost all writing benefits from being cut.

brilliant tip

If you're not used to using computers for writing, note that you don't have to hit 'return' at the end of each line. When you get to the end of a line, the program automatically 'wraps' your writing onto the next line for you.

Citations and references

It must be clear by now that you must cite authors and sources when you're discussing other people's ideas or quoting from their work. That's why you have to provide a reference list.

A citation is when you mention a source in the main body of your text. You usually note the surname of the author, date of publication and, in some styles, the relevant page(s). You'll give more details about it in the reference, details which, for example, the reader would need if she wanted to find it in a library.

brilliant examples

- A citation using the Harvard method would read like this:

  According to Smith (2005), there are three reasons why aardvark tongues are long.
- And, again using Harvard, the reference would be:

  Smith, J. V., 2005. Investigation of snout and tongue length in the African aardvark (*Orycteropus afer*). *Journal of Mammalian Research*, 34; 101–32.

Quoting numbers in text

The accepted conventions for including numbers in your writing are as follows:

- In general writing, spell out numbers from one to ten but use figures for 11 and above; in formal writing, spell them out from one to a hundred and use figures above that.
- Spell out high numbers that can be written in two words, such as 'six hundred' and when you get into the millions, you can combine figures and spelling. For example: 4,200,000 can also be written as 4.2 million.
- Always use figures for dates, times, currency or to give technical details ('5-amp fuse').
- Always spell out numbers that begin sentences, indefinite numbers ('hundreds of soldiers') or fractions ('seven-eighths').
- Numbers and fractions should be hyphenated, as in 'forty-three' or 'two-thirds'.

Figures and tables

If you need to use visual material or data to support your arguments, it's important that you do so in a way that best helps the reader to assimilate the information. Once again, there may be rules of presentation that are specific to your subject or department.

Figures

The term figures ('Fig.' for short) includes graphs, diagrams, charts, sketches, pictures and photographs (although sometimes photographs may be labelled as plates). The guidelines for using them are pretty strict, so it pays to know them.

- You must refer in the text to every figure you use. There are 'standard' wordings to use to do so, such as 'Fig. 4 shows that …'; or ' … results for one treatment were higher than for the other (see Fig. 2)'. Find what system applies in your area.
- Number the figures in the order in which you refer to them in the text. If you're including the figures themselves within

the main body of text (which usually makes things easier for the reader), put them at the next suitable position in the text after the first time you mention them.

- Try to print them at the top or bottom of a page, rather than between blocks of text. It looks neater and makes the text easier to read.

- Each figure should be labelled (the label is called the 'legend'). This'll include the number, a title and some text. The convention is for legends to appear below each figure.

When we were talking about constructing your written arguments, we kept stressing the need for clarity; the same obviously applies here. Make sure, for example, that the different slices of a pie chart or the lines and symbols in a graph are clearly distinguishable from one another. Be consistent by using the same line or shading for the same entity in all your figures. Colour printers are obviously an advantage here but some departments may still insist on black and white images. If you are using colour, keep it 'tasteful' and remember that certain combinations are difficult for some readers to differentiate.

There are technical reasons why some forms of data should be presented in particular ways (for example, proportional data is easier to read in a pie chart than in a line chart), but your main focus should always be on selecting a type of figure that will make it easiest for the reader assimilate the information.

brilliant tip

If you use integrated suites of office-type software, you can create graphs with the spreadsheet program and insert them directly into your word-processed text. You can even link the two so that, if you change the spreadsheet data, the change automatically appears in the graph in the text. To find out how this works, consult the manual or 'Help' facility in MS Word. Digital photographs can also be inserted using the 'Insert > Picture > From File' command.

Tables

Tables can summarise large amounts of detailed information, both descriptive and numerical. They generally include a number of columns and rows. Just as with graphs and charts, the convention is to put the categories on the vertical axis (in other words, down the page in the left-hand column), and the variables which are being measured on the horizontal axis (i.e. across the page at the top of the columns). So if we were presenting the data resulting from a survey of attitudes to university teaching, we might have rows for the opinions of students, lecturers, educational experts and the general public, and the columns across the page might be headed 'Positive aspects', 'Negative aspects', 'Value to society', 'Relevance to society'.

brilliant tip

If you have some data which could be presented as either a figure or a table, which should you choose? Well, first of all, never do both. The guiding principle should be to select whichever will be more likely to help the reader assimilate the information. If the message depends on visual impact, a figure might be best; but if details and numerical accuracy are important, a table might be more suitable.

brilliant dos and don'ts

Do

✔ Insert a single space after full stops, commas, colons, semicolons, closing inverted commas (double and single), question marks and exclamation marks.

✔ Create one standard line space between paragraphs.

✔ Italicise letters for foreign words and titles of books, journals and papers.

✔ Format headings in the same font size as the text, but in bold.

✔ Use the same figure and table styles that you find in your subject literature.

✔ Check your course handbook for specific presentational requirements.

Don't

✗ Choose flamboyance or ostentation. Go for the safe, standard word-processing layout conventions.

✗ Justify the text on both sides. Left-justified text creates more 'white space'.

✗ Insert a space after apostrophes 'inside' words, e.g. it's, men's, monkey's.

✗ Indent paragraphs. Go for the blocked style, separated by a double return.

✗ Automatically accept the graphical output from spreadsheets and other programs. They may not be in the approved style.

What next?

You may find that ...

... you have to submit written work with only your matriculation mark as an identifier. That's so that work can be marked anonymously. But pages can be lost and it may be difficult for the marker to know whether she has the complete piece of work. So do three basic things:

- staple all the sheets together
- use the View > header-footer function to insert your matriculation number in the footer
- add page numbers in the footer too.

Now each page is identifiable as yours and will remain in sequence. If you're not already in the habit of doing this, create an assignment writing template which does these things for you automatically. You can then use it for all your written coursework.

Check out the placing of tables and figures ...

... Look back at previous assignments to see whether you've been consistent in where and how you locate them. The Table > Properties command in Word lets you place visual elements to the left, right or centre of a page. Where you put them can affect how your reader perceives the information they're conveying.

brilliant recap

- Follow the prescribed academic conventions of presentation.
- Note the different types of layout for different subjects.
- The main elements of the layout are cover page, main text, font, margins, line spacing, paragraphs, sub-headings, word count, citations and references.
- Quote numbers in texts and use visual elements such as figures and tables.

CHAPTER 20

Making the most of feedback

Feedback comes in many forms: reactions to your contributions in tutorials from tutors and fellow students; discussions and questions about your point of view; and, of course, reactions – verbal and written – to the work you hand in for assessment. When essays are handed back, they usually have a mark on them and some comments. The comments may be in the margins or text and there's usually a general remark at the end. It's all too easy to jump to the grade and not take much notice of the remarks, but they can make a significant difference to your future grades and help to refine your writing and thinking.

Learning from feedback

There are two main types of assessment at university. The first are those where the grade you get doesn't get counted in your end-of-module mark, or counts for very little. They let you know what sort of standard you're reaching and often have a feedback sheet or comments written on them. The second are those which do count towards your final grade.

The simplest form of feedback is the mark itself. If it's good, you'll know you're reaching the required standard; if it's not, you'll know you need to do something to improve. If you're not sure how the grading system works, or what standards are expected, check your course or faculty handbooks. Even very early on, it might be worth trying to find out how your marks, whether they're given as percentages or in some other form, relate to the normal standard degree classes – first, upper second, lower second, third and unclassified.

If you're not sure why you got the mark you did or why the marker made a particular comment, it may be possible to arrange a meeting with him. Normally he'll be happy to explain it for you. But it's not a good idea to try to haggle over your marks. It's OK to point out that they've been added up wrongly, but otherwise, the mark is a genuine response on the part of the tutor to the quality of what you've written. Learn from it.

brilliant tip

Always read your feedback. It's there to point out specific aspects of your work which are being commended or aren't being handled as effectively as they could be. You should use it to make future submissions better, help to develop your structure and style, and deepen your understanding of the topic. If you ignore points that are made, especially those concerned with presentation or structure, you'll keep on repeating the mistakes and find yourself penalised for them over and over again.

Feedback comments and what they mean

As we indicated in Chapter 16, there's a set of signs which are used when proofreading to indicate various textual problems which need correcting. Unfortunately, when it comes to remarks written on your assignments, there isn't a verbal equivalent, i.e. a set terminology common to all lecturers and tutors. If there were, it would imply that both writing and marking are automatic processes with 'right' and 'wrong' answers. Markers may use the proofreading symbols as a sort of shorthand but their comments will be personal. So you'll need to get used to interpreting the particular ways they express their opinions. Also, if their habit is to scribble notes as they read, their handwriting may be difficult to decipher. Don't hesitate to ask if you can't understand what's being said.

Usually, comments are written in the right-hand margin or between the relevant lines. The words, phrases, sentences or paragraphs to which they refer are underlined, circled or indicated in some other way. All we can do here is give a few examples of commonly used feedback comments and suggest what they mean and how you should react to them to improve your writing.

Comments on content

- **Relevance? Importance? Value of example? So?**
  These suggest that you may have used a quotation that's not right for the context or you maybe haven't explained its relevance. Read your words carefully to test how logical they are and whether the irrelevance is obvious to you. Do you need to explain it further or more clearly? Should you choose a more appropriate example or quote?

- **Detail, Give more information, Example?, Too much detail/waffle/padding**
  You've either not provided enough detail to make your point or there's too much and your point's getting lost. You may also have realised that your argument's a bit thin so you've tried to make it seem better by putting in lots of description rather than analysis.

- **You could have included ..., What about ... ? Why didn't you ... ?**
  These obviously indicate that something's missing. You should, by reading through it, see where the gap is and what's needed to fill it.

- **Good! Excellent! ✓ (which may recur throughout the work)**
  These are the remarks you want – expressions of approval, confirmation that you're on the right track.

- **Poor, Weak, No! ✗ (which may recur throughout the work)**
  And this is what you don't want to see – expressions of disapproval, indications that there's something wrong with your examples, your quotations, your interpretation of them, etc.

Comments on structure

- **Logic?** *Non sequitur* **(which means this doesn't naturally follow what preceded it)**
  Your logic or argument is faulty. It may call for you to make quite radical changes to your approach to and analysis of the topic.

- **Where are you going with this? Unclear**
  This suggests that you've failed to introduce the topic clearly or that it's gone off course. Check that you do understand the task properly and know what restrictions there are on your response. Then decide how to tackle the subject.

- **Unbalanced discussion, Weak on pros and cons**
  Once again, it suggests a failure in your logic. When you're comparing and/or contrasting in any way, you must give more or less equal coverage to the pros and cons of the argument.

- **So what? Conclusion?**
  You've failed to conclude the essay clearly. You have to sum up the central features of your writing and shouldn't add any new material at this point. When you do that properly, it shows that you can think critically and define and highlight the main thread of your argument.

- **Watch out for over-quotation, Too many quotations**
  This means exactly what it says. If you include too many direct quotations from your sources, there's a real danger of plagiarism. You need to synthesise the information and reproduce the ideas in your own words to show that you've understood and absorbed it.

- **Move text (alternatively, loops and arrows may indicate the required changes)**
  Suggestions such as this are usually intended to improve the flow or the logic.

Comments on presentation

- **sp. (spelling), ⌐ (insert material here), ⌐ (break paragraph here), ⌐ (delete this material), P (punctuation error)**
  These are indications of minor proofing errors and this is where the proofreading symbols may be used.

- **Citations, Reference (required), Ref? Reference list omitted**
  You've missed out a reference to the original source of an idea, argument or quotation. It's a fault you must correct, otherwise you're once again risking plagiarism. If you provide no reference list, you'll lose marks because it suggests you've done no specialist reading.

- **Illegible! Untidy, Can't read**
  Again, this is self-evident. (It can also be ironic in that sometimes the marker's own handwriting is very untidy.) You can avoid it by using a word processor.

- **Please follow departmental template for reports, Order!**
  If the department or school provides a template for writing reports, you must use it. If you don't, you may lose marks.

> ☀ **brilliant** tip
>
> Don't just use the comments and advice on written coursework
> to improve your term-time work. Think of how you can use it
> constructively in exams. For example, if you're weak on structure,
> practise speed-planning answers to make them focused
> and succinct.

What next?

Look up and understand …

… your department or faculty's marking criteria. They'll help
you interpret feedback and understand how to reach the standard you want to achieve.

If your feedback comments …

… are frequently about the same sort of error, concentrate on
eliminating it. It may be spelling or grammar; they may suggest
you need more examples. Whatever the problem, spend time
identifying its exact nature and try to overcome it.

Give yourself feedback …

… This means reading your work as objectively as possible,
sensing where the weaknesses are and tackling them. It's the
sort of process that should be happening as you review and edit
your work and it's an essential academic skill.

Learn from …

… the views of your tutors. It's often natural to feel that some
feedback's unfair, harsh or has misunderstood your approach.
But the fact is that tutors usually have a deeper understanding of the topic than you do and, anyway, the harsh reality is

that, if you want to do well in a subject, you'd better find out what markers mean by 'good' answers and learn how to produce them.

brilliant recap

- There are various forms of feedback. It's important to take note of them.
- Know how to respond to the different written feedback comments on content, structure and presentation.

CHAPTER 21

Essays in exams

Most of what we've said about writing essays has been based on the idea that you have a decent period of time in which to do the various tasks. When you're confronted with essays in exams, the pressures are different and you need to adapt your techniques. This chapter contains suggestions as to what you might do to speed up the process of choosing and organising your material without sacrificing the quality of your answer.

What markers want

As well as having to perform quickly and well under pressure, you'll also have to do without help from dictionaries, thesauri and textbooks, and the time available for reviewing, editing and rewriting will be restricted. So let's start by thinking about what exam essays are for.

Multiple-choice or short-answer questions are mostly tests of your knowledge of a subject over a wide area. Essays, on the other hand, are looking for more depth and precision and they tend to relate to a limited issue. They expect you to develop an argument, explain alternative views or give lots of detail about the topic. They don't expect you to have that depth of knowledge about every aspect of your subject and so you usually get a choice of questions.

> ### brilliant tip
>
> We dealt with critical thinking at length in Chapter 7 but it's worth reminding you again of its importance and stressing that it's a vital skill in exam situations. As we've said, tutors expect you to think deeply about the question. And, of course, it may not actually be a question but an instruction of some sort such as those we listed in Chapter 3.
>
> In brief, you'll be asked to:
>
> * apply knowledge and understanding
> * analyse information
> * synthesise new ideas
> * evaluate issues, positions and arguments.

Planning the essay

First essential? Don't panic. Keep things simple and stay in control. Work quickly and use a concept diagram or mind map to start jotting down ideas relevant to the question. Allowing yourself some fast brainstorming of this sort will help you not only to think in terms of a linear approach (a leads to b leads to c, etc.) but also to have ideas which may be at a tangent to the main ones. In other words, do some lateral thinking, too, in order to open up different viewpoints. If you jot your plan down or make other notes in your exam book, that's fine, but make sure you cross them out before you hand in your paper. A single diagonal line will do.

Treat this phase seriously. Planning is essential. The temptation may be to get writing quickly and deal with structure as you go along but that's a recipe for a wandering, poorly developed argument.

Once you've made a note of everything that occurs to you, group ideas together to form an outline structure. Decide what's the best group to start with, which other groups it leads to, what contrasting, conflicting or supporting groups there are, and list the headings you're going to follow as you work through your answer. Remember the basic structure we described at the start:

- The introduction indicates briefly the overall context, what you'll be saying, and the approach you'll be taking.

- The main body carries the information, the argument and the main points of your answer.

- The conclusion sums up what you've said, confirms that you've done what the introduction promised, and puts the whole answer in a wider context.

brilliant tip

If you structure your answer well, that'll be reflected in the grade you get. But be prepared to be flexible too. Often, not just in exam situations but in other contexts, what you're writing (and thinking) changes as you go along – ideas generate other ideas, new directions and possibilities appear, you notice gaps in your argument. Don't discard your original plan – it's the basis on which you're building your answer, but be ready to adapt it as the new ideas occur.

brilliant dos and don'ts

Do

✔ Make sure you answer the question that's set, not one which resembles it and which you'd prefer. Consider the instruction words, the topic, the specific aspects you're asked to cover and any restrictions or limits it imposes.

▶

✔ Use part of the introduction to explain what *you* understand by the question. It'll help to focus your thinking and make your approach clear to the marker. But don't narrow it so much that you're excluding important elements.

✔ Plan your answer. It'll make the essay better and also help you to think more carefully about its relevance and logic.

Don't

✘ Repeat yourself or include irrelevant content. You'll be wasting time and it won't get you any extra marks. Use your plan to make sure you stick to the point.

✘ Leave 'white space' where you could jot down a few general points about a question which you're having trouble with. You may get a few marks for it which, added to the ones you get for your better answers, may help you pass.

✘ Make value judgements, i.e. statements that express unsupported personal views, often using subjective language.

✘ Use personal pronouns – 'I', 'you', 'we' and 'one'. Remember that this is an objective exercise.

Mistakes to avoid

There are many ways of losing marks in exams. Here's a list of those which occur most frequently:

● Not answering the question set.

● Poor time management. You know how much time you have for the number of questions, so use it sensibly. Don't spend ages on one question at the expense of others.

● Not noticing that one section of the paper carries more marks than another and allocating your time and effort accordingly.

- Failing to support your answer with relevant evidence or examples.

- Including basic facts or definitions which are so obvious that it's not necessary.

- Failing to illustrate an answer appropriately, perhaps by not drawing a relevant diagram, or drawing one that doesn't make things clearer.

- Giving incomplete or shallow answers because you don't know enough about the question or haven't thought it through properly.

- Waffling to fill space. Don't be tempted – it's always obvious to the marker that it's just padding.

- Illegible handwriting. If it can't be read, it can't be marked.

- Poor English, which obscures facts and ideas rather than expressing them clearly.

- An answer without obvious logic or structure to it.

- Factual errors.

- Failing to correct obvious mistakes which, if you organise your time properly and allow for proofreading, you'll be able to eliminate.

brilliant tip

Don't waste time or get bogged down trying to remember direct quotes word for word (unless they're essential, which may be the case in literature and law exams). Just give the sense of the quote, its relevance, and where it comes from.

⏵ brilliant examples

Here are some more illustrations of the sort of structural weaknesses to avoid in order to maximise your marks.

The magical mystery tour ...

... rambles on, drifting from point to disconnected point. It may have good stuff in it but it won't get many marks because it's not organised properly, its various parts don't connect with one another. In the end, it's incoherent. What it needs is structure.

The introduction and/or conclusion-free zone ...

... may have some good points in the main body but they haven't been introduced and no conclusions have been drawn about them. It's not enough to pile up facts, concepts and ideas, you've got to analyse them, think critically about them, deal with them at a deeper level to show you understand them. Your introduction and conclusion help to draw everything together.

The detail-overload syndrome ...

... crams information into the main body – some relevant, some not. So there's plenty of substance but very little structure and no distinction is made between the important and unimportant. This sort of answer suggests you may have remembered a lot but it doesn't show whether you've understood. It also indicates that you haven't read the question properly to find out exactly what's being asked for.

The stream of consciousness ...

... reads like a conversational monologue. There's little internal organisation, too few or too many signposting words, no real paragraphs and, if there is any logic, it's hard to follow. Good academic writing not only uses the right words, it structures them with care.

The waffly, irrelevant answer ...

... doesn't really tackle the question and just piles up whatever information is available without regard for the topic. You must analyse the instruction you're given and, on the basis of that, design a coherent answer plan. Irrelevant material won't earn any marks.

The half-answer ...

... deals with the first part of the question and doesn't seem to realise that there were more parts to address. Failing to answer the whole question could be disastrous because some parts could carry more marks than the one you concentrated on.

The rent-a-quote approach ...

... perhaps begins with a corny quote or is maybe littered with lots which have been clearly memorised especially for exams. They're not usually effective and they don't leave much room for any original thinking on the part of the writer. You're not marked for your memory but for what you do with the material you've absorbed.

Make time for reviewing your answers

After concentrating for a couple of hours or more, it's natural to want to get out of the exam room as soon as possible. But if you find there's still time left at the end, you should use every second of it to make sure you've maximised your chances of a good mark. Always plan to leave time for reviewing your answers. Spotting and correcting simple errors could mean the difference between a pass or a fail or between degree classifications. Make your review systematic.

- Make sure you haven't missed any of the basics. Check that you've numbered your answers properly, answered the right number of questions, and followed the instructions at the start of the paper.

- Check for spelling, grammar and sense. Read your answer critically, as if it had been written by someone else, and correct any obvious errors that strike you. Does it make sense? Do the sentences and paragraphs flow smoothly?

- And, yet again, make sure you've answered the question that was set and followed the instruction(s) in the title exactly, with nothing left out. Check to see that the different parts link together well and that there aren't any inconsistencies in your argument.

brilliant tip

The exam isn't a contest between you and the marker. Most lecturers would prefer to give out good grades, but they have to approach the marking process professionally and objectively. In fact, it's frustrating for them to see that a simple change of approach might have led to a better mark. They can't just assume you know and understand things unless you actually write them down.

A strategy for getting better marks

There's no substitute for effective revision, but being well prepared means more than memorising facts and concepts. You also need to arrive at the exam in the right state of mind, with a plan, a positive attitude and an eagerness to get started quickly and effectively. Part of your revision and preparation for the exam should be to get a good idea of the format to expect, and even an idea of some potential questions. In turn, this will enable you to work out some potential answer formats before the exam comes along, so you won't be starting answers completely from scratch.

When you've done your brainstorming, turn it into a plan as quickly as possible. Just find the headings of the various groups of ideas and number them in the order you'll be writing about them.

Keep your writing simple

It may be satisfying to find a great turn of phrase or some attention-grabbing prose, but not if it's using up valuable time. This isn't the same as coursework, where you have more leisure to refine your style. It's particularly important not to decorate the introduction with fine, sonorous phrases. Get to the point and get on with the answer. And get the balance right. Your introduction doesn't need to be very long. You'll earn most of your marks for the main body and conclusion, so spend more time and brainpower on them.

Use critical thinking

Remember that you'll get more marks for deeper thinking. Show that you've read around the subject and that you've not only retained information but understand and know how to use it. Make your answer analytical rather than descriptive. Don't just list facts. Look at all sides of a topic and draw a clear conclusion. This may involve evaluating two or more viewpoints, and either opting for one over the other or showing that they're equally valid or that neither is convincing.

Take care with presentation

Make sure you don't lose marks through poor presentation. Time pressure is intense throughout the exam, but if answers aren't legible and clearly laid out, they'll be marked down. If you keep getting feedback from tutors saying they're having problems reading your work, or that it's untidy, an obvious way of gaining some extra marks is to take their comments seriously and clean up your writing.

What next?

Look at questions ...

... in past exam papers, paying particular attention to the *depth* of answers required. Check the instruction word(s) and the context to see the level of thinking they're expecting.

Focus on definitions and possible formats ...

... as you're revising. If you find it hard to get your essays started during exams, it can help if you begin with a definition. Alternatively, you could set out the situation, the problem and then the potential solution. It depends on the question, of course, but if you're stuck, it'll at least give you something to base your thinking and writing on.

Use assessment exercises ...

... to improve your English. If you're not confident about how you use language, ask tutors how you might improve your marks and, if you're concerned that it might actually bring you down, go to the student advisory service. Lots of universities have academic writing advisors who can help with writing problems.

brilliant recap

- Understand what markers expect to see in essay answers in exams and plan your answers.
- Avoid the common types of mistakes students make in exams.
- Leave time at the end of your exam to review your answers carefully and thoroughly.
- A suggested strategy for getting better marks is to keep it simple, use critical thinking and take care with presentation.

Conclusion: take the advice but be yourself

We've covered a lot of ground and sometimes we've made the same points again and again: the need to avoid plagiarism and the associated importance of identifying and citing all your sources; the need to keep your academic style impersonal; the importance of making objective statements which you can support rather than offering value judgements; and many others. Our intention throughout has been to define the structures within which you need to work and help you to know why you're doing things in a particular way.

The idea isn't to turn you all into clones, regurgitating the same sort of thing, whatever your subject or wherever you are. Once you're comfortable with the different requirements of academic writing, you'll see them as liberating rather than restricting you. You'll use them to bring your own unique approach and interpretation to the various topics you're asked to consider.

But there's one theme which it's worth singling out for special reference – the need for you to exercise your critical thinking. That's the skill that will be most useful to you in everything you do. Life is far more than surfaces; if that's all you see and understand, you're missing subtleties, complexities, meanings that can change your appreciation of people, society, art, music, literature, commerce, politics, even nature itself. So get inside your studies and let them get inside you, look more deeply into the materials you encounter, be intellectually curious.

Don't accept all the information with which you're bombarded at its face value; unwrap it, question it, challenge it. Don't be content just to know things; understand them.